TABLE OF CONTENTS

INTRODUCTION TO THE LSAT

The Law School Admission Test is a half-day standardized test required for admission to all ABA-approved law schools, most Canadian law schools, and many other law schools. It consists of five 35-minute sections of multiple-choice questions. Four of the five sections contribute to the test taker's score. These sections include one reading comprehension section, one analytical reasoning section, and two logical reasoning sections. The unscored section, commonly referred to as the variable section, typically is used to pretest new test questions or to preequate new test forms. The placement of this section in the LSAT will vary. A 35-minute writing sample is administered at the end of the test. The writing sample is not scored by LSAC, but copies are sent to all law schools to which you apply. The score scale for the LSAT is 120 to 180.

The LSAT is designed to measure skills considered essential for success in law school: the reading and comprehension of complex texts with accuracy and insight; the organization and management of information and the ability to draw reasonable inferences from it; the ability to think critically; and the analysis and evaluation of the reasoning and arguments of others.

The LSAT provides a standard measure of acquired reading and verbal reasoning skills that law schools can use as one of several factors in assessing applicants.

For up-to-date information about LSAC's services, go to our website, LSAC.org.

SCORING

Your LSAT score is based on the number of questions you answer correctly (the raw score). There is no deduction for incorrect answers, and all questions count equally. In other words, there is no penalty for guessing.

Test Score Accuracy—Reliability and Standard Error of Measurement

Candidates perform at different levels on different occasions for reasons quite unrelated to the characteristics of a test itself. The accuracy of test scores is best described by the use of two related statistical terms: reliability and standard error of measurement.

Reliability is a measure of how consistently a test measures the skills being assessed. The higher the reliability coefficient for a test, the more certain we can be that test takers would get very similar scores if they took the test again.

LSAC reports an internal consistency measure of reliability for every test form. Reliability can vary from 0.00 to 1.00, and a test with no measurement error would have a reliability coefficient of 1.00 (never attained in practice). Reliability

coefficients for past LSAT forms have ranged from .90 to .95, indicating a high degree of consistency for these tests. LSAC expects the reliability of the LSAT to continue to fall within the same range.

LSAC also reports the amount of measurement error associated with each test form, a concept known as the standard error of measurement (SEM). The SEM, which is usually about 2.6 points, indicates how close a test taker's observed score is likely to be to his or her true score. True scores are theoretical scores that would be obtained from perfectly reliable tests with no measurement error—scores never known in practice.

Score bands, or ranges of scores that contain a test taker's true score a certain percentage of the time, can be derived using the SEM. LSAT score bands are constructed by adding and subtracting the (rounded) SEM to and from an actual LSAT score (e.g., the LSAT score, plus or minus 3 points). Scores near 120 or 180 have asymmetrical bands. Score bands constructed in this manner will contain an individual's true score approximately 68 percent of the time.

Measurement error also must be taken into account when comparing LSAT scores of two test takers. It is likely that small differences in scores are due to measurement error rather than to meaningful differences in ability. The standard error of score differences provides some guidance as to the importance of differences between two scores. The standard error of score differences is approximately 1.4 times larger than the standard error of measurement for the individual scores.

Thus, a test score should be regarded as a useful but approximate measure of a test taker's abilities as measured by the test, not as an exact determination of his or her abilities. LSAC encourages law schools to examine the range of scores within the interval that probably contains the test taker's true score (e.g., the test taker's score band) rather than solely interpret the reported score alone.

Adjustments for Variation in Test Difficulty

All test forms of the LSAT reported on the same score scale are designed to measure the same abilities, but one test form may be slightly easier or more difficult than another. The scores from different test forms are made comparable through a statistical procedure known as equating. As a result of equating, a given scaled score earned on different test forms reflects the same level of ability.

Research on the LSAT

Summaries of LSAT validity studies and other LSAT research can be found in member law school libraries and at LSAC.org.

To Inquire About Test Questions

If you find what you believe to be an error or ambiguity in a test question that affects your response to the question, contact LSAC by e-mail: LSATTS@LSAC.org, or write to Law School Admission Council, Test Development Group, Box 40, Newtown, PA 18940-0040.

HOW THIS PREPTEST DIFFERS FROM AN ACTUAL LSAT

This PrepTest is made up of the scored sections and writing sample from the actual disclosed LSAT administered in October 2010. However, it does not contain the extra, variable section that is used to pretest new test items of one of the three multiple-choice question types. The three multiple-choice question types may be in a different order in an actual LSAT than in this PrepTest. This is because the order of these question types is intentionally varied for each administration of the test.

THE THREE LSAT MULTIPLE-CHOICE QUESTION TYPES

The multiple-choice questions that make up most of the LSAT reflect a broad range of academic disciplines and are intended to give no advantage to candidates from a particular academic background.

The five sections of the test contain three different question types. The following material presents a general discussion of the nature of each question type and some strategies that can be used in answering them.

Analytical Reasoning Questions

Analytical Reasoning questions are designed to assess the ability to consider a group of facts and rules, and, given those facts and rules, determine what could or must be true. The specific scenarios associated with these questions are usually unrelated to law, since they are intended to be accessible to a wide range of test takers. However, the skills tested parallel those involved in determining what could or must be the case given a set of regulations, the terms of a contract, or the facts of a legal case in relation to the law. In Analytical Reasoning questions, you are asked to reason deductively from a set of statements and rules or principles that describe relationships among persons, things, or events.

Analytical Reasoning questions appear in sets, with each set based on a single passage. The passage used for each set of questions describes common ordering relationships or grouping relationships, or a combination of both types of relationships. Examples include scheduling employees for work shifts, assigning instructors to class sections,

ordering tasks according to priority, and distributing grants for projects.

Analytical Reasoning questions test a range of deductive reasoning skills. These include:

- Comprehending the basic structure of a set of relationships by determining a complete solution to the problem posed (for example, an acceptable seating arrangement of all six diplomats around a table)

- Reasoning with conditional ("if-then") statements and recognizing logically equivalent formulations of such statements

- Inferring what could be true or must be true from given facts and rules

- Inferring what could be true or must be true from given facts and rules together with new information in the form of an additional or substitute fact or rule

- Recognizing when two statements are logically equivalent in context by identifying a condition or rule that could replace one of the original conditions while still resulting in the same possible outcomes

Analytical Reasoning questions reflect the kinds of detailed analyses of relationships and sets of constraints that a law student must perform in legal problem solving. For example, an Analytical Reasoning passage might describe six diplomats being seated around a table, following certain rules of protocol as to who can sit where. You, the test taker, must answer questions about the logical implications of given and new information. For example, you may be asked who can sit between diplomats X and Y, or who cannot sit next to X if W sits next to Y. Similarly, if you were a student in law school, you might be asked to analyze a scenario involving a set of particular circumstances and a set of governing rules in the form of constitutional provisions, statutes, administrative codes, or prior rulings that have been upheld. You might then be asked to determine the legal options in the scenario: what is required given the scenario, what is permissible given the scenario, and what is prohibited given the scenario. Or you might be asked to develop a "theory" for the case: when faced with an incomplete set of facts about the case, you must fill in the picture based on what is implied by the facts that are known. The problem could be elaborated by the addition of new information or hypotheticals.

No formal training in logic is required to answer these questions correctly. Analytical Reasoning questions are intended to be answered using knowledge, skills, and reasoning ability generally expected of college students and graduates.

Suggested Approach

Some people may prefer to answer first those questions about a passage that seem less difficult and then those that seem more difficult. In general, it is best to finish one passage before starting on another, because much time can be lost in returning to a passage and reestablishing familiarity with its relationships. However, if you are having great difficulty on one particular set of questions and are spending too much time on them, it may be to your advantage to skip that set of questions and go on to the next passage, returning to the problematic set of questions after you have finished the other questions in the section.

Do not assume that because the conditions for a set of questions look long or complicated, the questions based on those conditions will be especially difficult.

Read the passage carefully. Careful reading and analysis are necessary to determine the exact nature of the relationships involved in an Analytical Reasoning passage. Some relationships are fixed (for example, P and R must always work on the same project). Other relationships are variable (for example, Q must be assigned to either team 1 or team 3). Some relationships that are not stated explicitly in the conditions are implied by and can be deduced from those that are stated (for example, if one condition about paintings in a display specifies that Painting K must be to the left of Painting Y, and another specifies that Painting W must be to the left of Painting K, then it can be deduced that Painting W must be to the left of Painting Y).

In reading the conditions, do not introduce unwarranted assumptions. For instance, in a set of questions establishing relationships of height and weight among the members of a team, do not assume that a person who is taller than another person must weigh more than that person. As another example, suppose a set involves ordering and a question in the set asks what must be true if both X and Y must be earlier than Z; in this case, do not assume that X must be earlier than Y merely because X is mentioned before Y. All the information needed to answer each question is provided in the passage and the question itself.

The conditions are designed to be as clear as possible. Do not interpret the conditions as if they were intended to trick you. For example, if a question asks how many people could be eligible to serve on a committee, consider only those people named in the passage unless directed otherwise. When in doubt, read the conditions in their most obvious sense. Remember, however, that the language in the conditions is intended to be read for precise meaning. It is essential to pay particular attention to words that describe or limit relationships, such as "only," "exactly," "never," "always," "must be," "cannot be," and the like.

The result of this careful reading will be a clear picture of the structure of the relationships involved, including the kinds of relationships permitted, the participants in the relationships, and the range of possible actions or attributes for these participants.

Keep in mind question independence. Each question should be considered separately from the other questions in its set. No information, except what is given in the original conditions, should be carried over from one question to another.

In some cases a question will simply ask for conclusions to be drawn from the conditions as originally given. Some questions may, however, add information to the original conditions or temporarily suspend or replace one of the original conditions for the purpose of that question only. For example, if Question 1 adds the supposition "if P is sitting at table 2 …," this supposition should NOT be carried over to any other question in the set.

Consider highlighting text and using diagrams. Many people find it useful to underline key points in the passage and in each question. In addition, it may prove very helpful to draw a diagram to assist you in finding the solution to the problem.

In preparing for the test, you may wish to experiment with different types of diagrams. For a scheduling problem, a simple calendar-like diagram may be helpful. For a grouping problem, an array of labeled columns or rows may be useful.

Even though most people find diagrams to be very helpful, some people seldom use them, and for some individual questions no one will need a diagram. There is by no means universal agreement on which kind of diagram is best for which problem or in which cases a diagram is most useful. Do not be concerned if a particular problem in the test seems to be best approached without the use of a diagram.

Logical Reasoning Questions

Arguments are a fundamental part of the law, and analyzing arguments is a key element of legal analysis. Training in the law builds on a foundation of basic reasoning skills. Law students must draw on the skills of analyzing, evaluating, constructing, and refuting arguments. They need to be able to identify what information is relevant to an issue or argument and what impact further evidence might have. They need to be able to reconcile opposing positions and use arguments to persuade others.

Logical Reasoning questions evaluate the ability to analyze, critically evaluate, and complete arguments as they occur in ordinary language. The questions are based on short arguments drawn from a wide variety of sources, including newspapers, general interest magazines, scholarly publications, advertisements, and informal discourse. These arguments mirror legal reasoning in the types of arguments presented and in their complexity, though few of the arguments actually have law as a subject matter.

Each Logical Reasoning question requires you to read and comprehend a short passage, then answer one question (or, rarely, two questions) about it. The questions are designed to assess a wide range of skills involved in thinking critically, with an emphasis on skills that are central to legal reasoning.

These skills include:

- Recognizing the parts of an argument and their relationships

- Recognizing similarities and differences between patterns of reasoning

- Drawing well-supported conclusions

- Reasoning by analogy

- Recognizing misunderstandings or points of disagreement

- Determining how additional evidence affects an argument

- Detecting assumptions made by particular arguments

- Identifying and applying principles or rules

- Identifying flaws in arguments

- Identifying explanations

The questions do not presuppose specialized knowledge of logical terminology. For example, you will not be expected to know the meaning of specialized terms such as "ad hominem" or "syllogism." On the other hand, you will be expected to understand and critique the reasoning contained in arguments. This requires that you possess a university-level understanding of widely used concepts such as argument, premise, assumption, and conclusion.

Suggested Approach

Read each question carefully. Make sure that you understand the meaning of each part of the question. Make sure that you understand the meaning of each answer choice and the ways in which it may or may not relate to the question posed.

Do not pick a response simply because it is a true statement. Although true, it may not answer the question posed.

Answer each question on the basis of the information that is given, even if you do not agree with it. Work within the context provided by the passage. LSAT questions do not involve any tricks or hidden meanings.

Reading Comprehension Questions

Both law school and the practice of law revolve around extensive reading of highly varied, dense, argumentative, and expository texts (for example, cases, codes, contracts, briefs, decisions, evidence). This reading must be exacting, distinguishing precisely what is said from what is not said. It involves comparison, analysis, synthesis, and application (for example, of principles and rules). It involves drawing appropriate inferences and applying ideas and arguments to new contexts. Law school reading also requires the ability to grasp unfamiliar subject matter and the ability to penetrate difficult and challenging material.

The purpose of LSAT Reading Comprehension questions is to measure the ability to read, with understanding and insight, examples of lengthy and complex materials similar to those commonly encountered in law school. The Reading Comprehension section of the LSAT contains four sets of reading questions, each set consisting of a selection of reading material followed by five to eight questions. The reading selection in three of the four sets consists of a single reading passage; the other set contains two related shorter passages. Sets with two passages are a variant of Reading Comprehension called Comparative Reading, which was introduced in June 2007.

Comparative Reading questions concern the relationships between the two passages, such as those of generalization/instance, principle/application, or point/counterpoint. Law school work often requires reading two or more texts in conjunction with each other and understanding their relationships. For example, a law student may read a trial court decision together with an appellate court decision that overturns it, or identify the fact pattern from a hypothetical suit together with the potentially controlling case law.

Reading selections for LSAT Reading Comprehension questions are drawn from a wide range of subjects in the humanities, the social sciences, the biological and physical sciences, and areas related to the law. Generally, the selections are densely written, use high-level vocabulary, and contain sophisticated argument or complex rhetorical structure (for example, multiple points of view). Reading Comprehension questions require you to read carefully and accurately, to determine the relationships among the various parts of the reading selection, and to draw reasonable inferences from the material in the selection. The questions may ask about the following characteristics of a passage or pair of passages:

- The main idea or primary purpose

- Information that is explicitly stated

- Information or ideas that can be inferred

- The meaning or purpose of words or phrases as used in context

- The organization or structure

- The application of information in the selection to a new context

- Principles that function in the selection

- Analogies to claims or arguments in the selection

- An author's attitude as revealed in the tone of a passage or the language used

- The impact of new information on claims or arguments in the selection

Suggested Approach

Since reading selections are drawn from many different disciplines and sources, you should not be discouraged if you encounter material with which you are not familiar. It is important to remember that questions are to be answered exclusively on the basis of the information provided in the selection. There is no particular knowledge that you are expected to bring to the test, and you should not make inferences based on any prior knowledge of a subject that you may have. You may, however, wish to defer working on a set of questions that seems particularly difficult or unfamiliar until after you have dealt with sets you find easier.

Strategies. One question that often arises in connection with Reading Comprehension has to do with the most effective and efficient order in which to read the selections and questions. Possible approaches include:

- reading the selection very closely and then answering the questions;

- reading the questions first, reading the selection closely, and then returning to the questions; or

- skimming the selection and questions very quickly, then rereading the selection closely and answering the questions.

Test takers are different, and the best strategy for one might not be the best strategy for another. In preparing for the test, therefore, you might want to experiment with the different strategies and decide what works most effectively for you.

Remember that your strategy must be effective under timed conditions. For this reason, the first strategy—reading the selection very closely and then answering the questions—may be the most effective for you. Nonetheless, if you believe that one of the other strategies

might be more effective for you, you should try it out and assess your performance using it.

Reading the selection. Whatever strategy you choose, you should give the passage or pair of passages at least one careful reading before answering the questions. Try to distinguish main ideas from supporting ideas, and opinions or attitudes from factual, objective information. Note transitions from one idea to the next and identify the relationships among the different ideas or parts of a passage, or between the two passages in comparative reading sets. Consider how and why an author makes points and draws conclusions. Be sensitive to implications of what the passages say.

You may find it helpful to mark key parts of passages. For example, you might underline main ideas or important arguments, and you might circle transitional words—"although," "nevertheless," "correspondingly," and the like—that will help you map the structure of a passage. Also, you might note descriptive words that will help you identify an author's attitude toward a particular idea or person.

Answering the Questions

- Always read all the answer choices before selecting the best answer. The best answer choice is the one that most accurately and completely answers the question being posed.

- Respond to the specific question being asked. Do not pick an answer choice simply because it is a true statement. For example, picking a true statement might yield an incorrect answer to a question in which you are asked to identify an author's position on an issue, since you are not being asked to evaluate the truth of the author's position but only to correctly identify what that position is.

- Answer the questions only on the basis of the information provided in the selection. Your own views, interpretations, or opinions, and those you have heard from others, may sometimes conflict with those expressed in a reading selection; however, you are expected to work within the context provided by the reading selection. You should not expect to agree with everything you encounter in reading comprehension passages.

THE WRITING SAMPLE

On the day of the test, you will be asked to write one sample essay. LSAC does not score the writing sample, but copies are sent to all law schools to which you apply. According to a 2006 LSAC survey of 157 United States and Canadian law schools, almost all use the writing sample in evaluating at least some applications for admission. Failure to respond to writing sample prompts and frivolous responses have been used by law schools as grounds for rejection of applications for admission.

In developing and implementing the writing sample portion of the LSAT, LSAC has operated on the following premises: First, law schools and the legal profession value highly the ability to communicate effectively in writing. Second, it is important to encourage potential law students to develop effective writing skills. Third, a sample of an applicant's writing, produced under controlled conditions, is a potentially useful indication of that person's writing ability. Fourth, the writing sample can serve as an independent check on other writing submitted by applicants as part of the admission process. Finally, writing samples may be useful for diagnostic purposes related to improving a candidate's writing.

The writing prompt presents a decision problem. You are asked to make a choice between two positions or courses of action. Both of the choices are defensible, and you are given criteria and facts on which to base your decision. There is no "right" or "wrong" position to take on the topic, so the quality of each test taker's response is a function not of which choice is made, but of how well or poorly the choice is supported and how well or poorly the other choice is criticized.

The LSAT writing prompt was designed and validated by legal education professionals. Since it involves writing based on fact sets and criteria, the writing sample gives applicants the opportunity to demonstrate the type of argumentative writing that is required in law school, although the topics are usually nonlegal.

You will have 35 minutes in which to plan and write an essay on the topic you receive. Read the topic and the accompanying directions carefully. You will probably find it best to spend a few minutes considering the topic and organizing your thoughts before you begin writing. In your essay, be sure to develop your ideas fully, leaving time, if possible, to review what you have written. Do not write on a topic other than the one specified. Writing on a topic of your own choice is not acceptable.

No special knowledge is required or expected for this writing exercise. Law schools are interested in the reasoning, clarity, organization, language usage, and writing mechanics displayed in your essay. How well you write is more important than how much you write. Confine your essay to the blocked, lined area on the front and back of the separate Writing Sample Response Sheet. Only that area will be reproduced for law schools. Be sure that your writing is legible.

TAKING THE PREPTEST UNDER SIMULATED LSAT CONDITIONS

One important way to prepare for the LSAT is to simulate the day of the test by taking a practice test under actual time constraints. Taking a practice test under timed conditions helps you to estimate the amount of time you can afford to spend on each question in a section and to determine the question types on which you may need additional practice.

Since the LSAT is a timed test, it is important to use your allotted time wisely. During the test, you may work only on the section designated by the test supervisor. You can-not devote extra time to a difficult section and make up that time on a section you find easier. In pacing yourself, and checking your answers, you should think of each section of the test as a separate minitest.

Be sure that you answer every question on the test. When you do not know the correct answer to a question, first eliminate the responses that you know are incorrect, then make your best guess among the remaining choices. Do not be afraid to guess as there is no penalty for incorrect answers.

When you take a practice test, abide by all the requirements specified in the directions and keep strictly within the specified time limits. Work without a rest period. When you take an actual test, you will have only a short break—usually 10–15 minutes—after SECTION III.

When taken under conditions as much like actual testing conditions as possible, a practice test provides very useful preparation for taking the LSAT.

Official directions for the four multiple-choice sections and the writing sample are included in this PrepTest so that you can approximate actual testing conditions as you practice.

To take the test:

- Set a timer for 35 minutes. Answer all the questions in SECTION I of this PrepTest. Stop working on that section when the 35 minutes have elapsed.

- Repeat, allowing yourself 35 minutes each for sections II, III, and IV.

- Set the timer again for 35 minutes, then prepare your response to the writing sample topic at the end of this PrepTest.

- Refer to "Computing Your Score" for the PrepTest for instruction on evaluating your performance. An answer key is provided for that purpose.

The practice test that follows consists of four sections corresponding to the four scored sections of the December 2010 LSAT. Also reprinted is the December 2010 unscored writing sample topic.

General Directions for the LSAT Answer Sheet

The actual testing time for this portion of the test will be 2 hours 55 minutes. There are five sections, each with a time limit of 35 minutes. The supervisor will tell you when to begin and end each section. If you finish a section before time is called, you may check your work on that section only; do not turn to any other section of the test book and do not work on any other section either in the test book or on the answer sheet.

There are several different types of questions on the test, and each question type has its own directions. Be sure you understand the directions for each question type before attempting to answer any questions in that section.

Not everyone will finish all the questions in the time allowed. Do not hurry, but work steadily and as quickly as you can without sacrificing accuracy. You are advised to use your time effectively. If a question seems too difficult, go on to the next one and return to the difficult question after completing the section. MARK THE BEST ANSWER YOU CAN FOR EVERY QUESTION. NO DEDUCTIONS WILL BE MADE FOR WRONG ANSWERS. YOUR SCORE WILL BE BASED ONLY ON THE NUMBER OF QUESTIONS YOU ANSWER CORRECTLY.

ALL YOUR ANSWERS MUST BE MARKED ON THE ANSWER SHEET. Answer spaces for each question are lettered to correspond with the letters of the potential answers to each question in the test book. After you have decided which of the answers is correct, blacken the corresponding space on the answer sheet. BE SURE THAT EACH MARK IS BLACK AND COMPLETELY FILLS THE ANSWER SPACE. Give only one answer to each question. If you change an answer, be sure that all previous marks are erased completely. Since the answer sheet is machine scored, incomplete erasures may be interpreted as intended answers. ANSWERS RECORDED IN THE TEST BOOK WILL NOT BE SCORED.

There may be more questions noted on this answer sheet than there are questions in a section. Do not be concerned but be certain that the section and number of the question you are answering matches the answer sheet section and question number. Additional answer spaces in any answer sheet section should be left blank. Begin your next section in the number one answer space for that section.

LSAC takes various steps to ensure that answer sheets are returned from test centers in a timely manner for processing. In the unlikely event that an answer sheet(s) is not received, LSAC will permit the examinee to either retest at no additional fee or to receive a refund of his or her LSAT fee. THESE REMEDIES ARE THE EXCLUSIVE REMEDIES AVAILABLE IN THE UNLIKELY EVENT THAT AN ANSWER SHEET IS NOT RECEIVED BY LSAC.

Score Cancellation

Complete this section only if you are absolutely certain you want to cancel your score. A CANCELLATION REQUEST CANNOT BE RESCINDED. IF YOU ARE AT ALL UNCERTAIN, YOU SHOULD NOT COMPLETE THIS SECTION.

To cancel your score from this administration, you **must:**

A. fill in both ovals here ..... ○ ○

   AND

B. read the following statement. Then sign your name and enter the date.
   YOUR SIGNATURE ALONE IS NOT SUFFICIENT FOR SCORE CANCELLATION. BOTH OVALS ABOVE MUST BE FILLED IN FOR SCANNING EQUIPMENT TO RECOGNIZE YOUR REQUEST FOR SCORE CANCELLATION.

   I certify that I wish to cancel my test score from this administration. I understand that my request is irreversible and that my score will not be sent to me or to the law schools to which I apply.

_____
Sign your name in full

_____
Date

FOR LSAC USE ONLY ●

HOW DID YOU PREPARE FOR THE LSAT?
(Select all that apply.)

Responses to this item are voluntary and will be used for statistical research purposes only.

- ○ By studying the free sample questions available on LSAC's website.
- ○ By taking the free sample LSAT available on LSAC's website.
- ○ By working through official LSAT *PrepTests, ItemWise,* and/or other LSAC test prep products.
- ○ By using LSAT prep books or software **not** published by LSAC.
- ○ By attending a commercial test preparation or coaching course.
- ○ By attending a test preparation or coaching course offered through an undergraduate institution.
- ○ Self study.
- ○ Other preparation.
- ○ No preparation.

CERTIFYING STATEMENT

Please write the following statement. Sign and date.

I certify that I am the examinee whose name appears on this answer sheet and that I am here to take the LSAT for the sole purpose of being considered for admission to law school. I further certify that I will neither assist nor receive assistance from any other candidate, and I agree not to copy or retain examination questions or to transmit them to or discuss them with any other person in any form.

_____
_____
_____
_____
_____
_____
_____
_____
_____
_____

SIGNATURE: _____   TODAY'S DATE: ___/___/___
                                                                  MONTH DAY YEAR

INSTRUCTIONS FOR COMPLETING THE BIOGRAPHICAL AREA ARE ON THE BACK COVER OF YOUR TEST BOOKLET

USE ONLY A NO. 2 OR HB PENCIL TO COMPLETE THIS ANSWER SHEET. DO NOT USE INK.

A

USE A NO. 2 OR HB PENCIL ONLY

● Right Mark   ⊘ ⊗ ⊙ **Wrong Marks**

1 LAST NAME / FIRST NAME / MI

2 SOCIAL SECURITY/ SOCIAL INSURANCE NO.

3 LSAC ACCOUNT NUMBER   L

4 DATE OF BIRTH

MONTH	DAY	YEAR
Jan		
Feb		
Mar		
Apr		
May		
June		
July		
Aug		
Sept		
Oct		
Nov		
Dec		

5 RACIAL/ETHNIC DESCRIPTION
Mark one or more

- ○ 1 Aboriginal/TSI Australian
- ○ 2 Amer. Indian/Alaska Native
- ○ 3 Asian
- ○ 4 Black/African American
- ○ 5 Canadian Aboriginal
- ○ 6 Caucasian/White
- ○ 7 Hispanic/Latino
- ○ 8 Native Hawaiian/ Other Pacific Islander
- ○ 9 Puerto Rican

6 GENDER
- ○ Male
- ○ Female

7 DOMINANT LANGUAGE
- ○ English
- ○ Other

8 ENGLISH FLUENCY
- ○ Yes   ○ No

9 TEST BOOK SERIAL NO.

10 TEST FORM

11 TEST DATE

MONTH / DAY / YEAR

12 CENTER NUMBER

13 TEST FORM COD

Law School Admission Test

Mark one and only one answer to each question. Be sure to fill in completely the space for your intended answer choice. If you erase, do so completely. Make no stray marks.

SECTION 1	SECTION 2	SECTION 3	SECTION 4	SECTION 5
1 Ⓐ Ⓑ Ⓒ Ⓓ Ⓔ	1 Ⓐ Ⓑ Ⓒ Ⓓ Ⓔ	1 Ⓐ Ⓑ Ⓒ Ⓓ Ⓔ	1 Ⓐ Ⓑ Ⓒ Ⓓ Ⓔ	1 Ⓐ Ⓑ Ⓒ Ⓓ Ⓔ
2 Ⓐ Ⓑ Ⓒ Ⓓ Ⓔ	2 Ⓐ Ⓑ Ⓒ Ⓓ Ⓔ	2 Ⓐ Ⓑ Ⓒ Ⓓ Ⓔ	2 Ⓐ Ⓑ Ⓒ Ⓓ Ⓔ	2 Ⓐ Ⓑ Ⓒ Ⓓ Ⓔ
3 Ⓐ Ⓑ Ⓒ Ⓓ Ⓔ	3 Ⓐ Ⓑ Ⓒ Ⓓ Ⓔ	3 Ⓐ Ⓑ Ⓒ Ⓓ Ⓔ	3 Ⓐ Ⓑ Ⓒ Ⓓ Ⓔ	3 Ⓐ Ⓑ Ⓒ Ⓓ Ⓔ
4 Ⓐ Ⓑ Ⓒ Ⓓ Ⓔ	4 Ⓐ Ⓑ Ⓒ Ⓓ Ⓔ	4 Ⓐ Ⓑ Ⓒ Ⓓ Ⓔ	4 Ⓐ Ⓑ Ⓒ Ⓓ Ⓔ	4 Ⓐ Ⓑ Ⓒ Ⓓ Ⓔ
5 Ⓐ Ⓑ Ⓒ Ⓓ Ⓔ	5 Ⓐ Ⓑ Ⓒ Ⓓ Ⓔ	5 Ⓐ Ⓑ Ⓒ Ⓓ Ⓔ	5 Ⓐ Ⓑ Ⓒ Ⓓ Ⓔ	5 Ⓐ Ⓑ Ⓒ Ⓓ Ⓔ
6 Ⓐ Ⓑ Ⓒ Ⓓ Ⓔ	6 Ⓐ Ⓑ Ⓒ Ⓓ Ⓔ	6 Ⓐ Ⓑ Ⓒ Ⓓ Ⓔ	6 Ⓐ Ⓑ Ⓒ Ⓓ Ⓔ	6 Ⓐ Ⓑ Ⓒ Ⓓ Ⓔ
7 Ⓐ Ⓑ Ⓒ Ⓓ Ⓔ	7 Ⓐ Ⓑ Ⓒ Ⓓ Ⓔ	7 Ⓐ Ⓑ Ⓒ Ⓓ Ⓔ	7 Ⓐ Ⓑ Ⓒ Ⓓ Ⓔ	7 Ⓐ Ⓑ Ⓒ Ⓓ Ⓔ
8 Ⓐ Ⓑ Ⓒ Ⓓ Ⓔ	8 Ⓐ Ⓑ Ⓒ Ⓓ Ⓔ	8 Ⓐ Ⓑ Ⓒ Ⓓ Ⓔ	8 Ⓐ Ⓑ Ⓒ Ⓓ Ⓔ	8 Ⓐ Ⓑ Ⓒ Ⓓ Ⓔ
9 Ⓐ Ⓑ Ⓒ Ⓓ Ⓔ	9 Ⓐ Ⓑ Ⓒ Ⓓ Ⓔ	9 Ⓐ Ⓑ Ⓒ Ⓓ Ⓔ	9 Ⓐ Ⓑ Ⓒ Ⓓ Ⓔ	9 Ⓐ Ⓑ Ⓒ Ⓓ Ⓔ
10 Ⓐ Ⓑ Ⓒ Ⓓ Ⓔ	10 Ⓐ Ⓑ Ⓒ Ⓓ Ⓔ	10 Ⓐ Ⓑ Ⓒ Ⓓ Ⓔ	10 Ⓐ Ⓑ Ⓒ Ⓓ Ⓔ	10 Ⓐ Ⓑ Ⓒ Ⓓ Ⓔ
11 Ⓐ Ⓑ Ⓒ Ⓓ Ⓔ	11 Ⓐ Ⓑ Ⓒ Ⓓ Ⓔ	11 Ⓐ Ⓑ Ⓒ Ⓓ Ⓔ	11 Ⓐ Ⓑ Ⓒ Ⓓ Ⓔ	11 Ⓐ Ⓑ Ⓒ Ⓓ Ⓔ
12 Ⓐ Ⓑ Ⓒ Ⓓ Ⓔ	12 Ⓐ Ⓑ Ⓒ Ⓓ Ⓔ	12 Ⓐ Ⓑ Ⓒ Ⓓ Ⓔ	12 Ⓐ Ⓑ Ⓒ Ⓓ Ⓔ	12 Ⓐ Ⓑ Ⓒ Ⓓ Ⓔ
13 Ⓐ Ⓑ Ⓒ Ⓓ Ⓔ	13 Ⓐ Ⓑ Ⓒ Ⓓ Ⓔ	13 Ⓐ Ⓑ Ⓒ Ⓓ Ⓔ	13 Ⓐ Ⓑ Ⓒ Ⓓ Ⓔ	13 Ⓐ Ⓑ Ⓒ Ⓓ Ⓔ
14 Ⓐ Ⓑ Ⓒ Ⓓ Ⓔ	14 Ⓐ Ⓑ Ⓒ Ⓓ Ⓔ	14 Ⓐ Ⓑ Ⓒ Ⓓ Ⓔ	14 Ⓐ Ⓑ Ⓒ Ⓓ Ⓔ	14 Ⓐ Ⓑ Ⓒ Ⓓ Ⓔ
15 Ⓐ Ⓑ Ⓒ Ⓓ Ⓔ	15 Ⓐ Ⓑ Ⓒ Ⓓ Ⓔ	15 Ⓐ Ⓑ Ⓒ Ⓓ Ⓔ	15 Ⓐ Ⓑ Ⓒ Ⓓ Ⓔ	15 Ⓐ Ⓑ Ⓒ Ⓓ Ⓔ
16 Ⓐ Ⓑ Ⓒ Ⓓ Ⓔ	16 Ⓐ Ⓑ Ⓒ Ⓓ Ⓔ	16 Ⓐ Ⓑ Ⓒ Ⓓ Ⓔ	16 Ⓐ Ⓑ Ⓒ Ⓓ Ⓔ	16 Ⓐ Ⓑ Ⓒ Ⓓ Ⓔ
17 Ⓐ Ⓑ Ⓒ Ⓓ Ⓔ	17 Ⓐ Ⓑ Ⓒ Ⓓ Ⓔ	17 Ⓐ Ⓑ Ⓒ Ⓓ Ⓔ	17 Ⓐ Ⓑ Ⓒ Ⓓ Ⓔ	17 Ⓐ Ⓑ Ⓒ Ⓓ Ⓔ
18 Ⓐ Ⓑ Ⓒ Ⓓ Ⓔ	18 Ⓐ Ⓑ Ⓒ Ⓓ Ⓔ	18 Ⓐ Ⓑ Ⓒ Ⓓ Ⓔ	18 Ⓐ Ⓑ Ⓒ Ⓓ Ⓔ	18 Ⓐ Ⓑ Ⓒ Ⓓ Ⓔ
19 Ⓐ Ⓑ Ⓒ Ⓓ Ⓔ	19 Ⓐ Ⓑ Ⓒ Ⓓ Ⓔ	19 Ⓐ Ⓑ Ⓒ Ⓓ Ⓔ	19 Ⓐ Ⓑ Ⓒ Ⓓ Ⓔ	19 Ⓐ Ⓑ Ⓒ Ⓓ Ⓔ
20 Ⓐ Ⓑ Ⓒ Ⓓ Ⓔ	20 Ⓐ Ⓑ Ⓒ Ⓓ Ⓔ	20 Ⓐ Ⓑ Ⓒ Ⓓ Ⓔ	20 Ⓐ Ⓑ Ⓒ Ⓓ Ⓔ	20 Ⓐ Ⓑ Ⓒ Ⓓ Ⓔ
21 Ⓐ Ⓑ Ⓒ Ⓓ Ⓔ	21 Ⓐ Ⓑ Ⓒ Ⓓ Ⓔ	21 Ⓐ Ⓑ Ⓒ Ⓓ Ⓔ	21 Ⓐ Ⓑ Ⓒ Ⓓ Ⓔ	21 Ⓐ Ⓑ Ⓒ Ⓓ Ⓔ
22 Ⓐ Ⓑ Ⓒ Ⓓ Ⓔ	22 Ⓐ Ⓑ Ⓒ Ⓓ Ⓔ	22 Ⓐ Ⓑ Ⓒ Ⓓ Ⓔ	22 Ⓐ Ⓑ Ⓒ Ⓓ Ⓔ	22 Ⓐ Ⓑ Ⓒ Ⓓ Ⓔ
23 Ⓐ Ⓑ Ⓒ Ⓓ Ⓔ	23 Ⓐ Ⓑ Ⓒ Ⓓ Ⓔ	23 Ⓐ Ⓑ Ⓒ Ⓓ Ⓔ	23 Ⓐ Ⓑ Ⓒ Ⓓ Ⓔ	23 Ⓐ Ⓑ Ⓒ Ⓓ Ⓔ
24 Ⓐ Ⓑ Ⓒ Ⓓ Ⓔ	24 Ⓐ Ⓑ Ⓒ Ⓓ Ⓔ	24 Ⓐ Ⓑ Ⓒ Ⓓ Ⓔ	24 Ⓐ Ⓑ Ⓒ Ⓓ Ⓔ	24 Ⓐ Ⓑ Ⓒ Ⓓ Ⓔ
25 Ⓐ Ⓑ Ⓒ Ⓓ Ⓔ	25 Ⓐ Ⓑ Ⓒ Ⓓ Ⓔ	25 Ⓐ Ⓑ Ⓒ Ⓓ Ⓔ	25 Ⓐ Ⓑ Ⓒ Ⓓ Ⓔ	25 Ⓐ Ⓑ Ⓒ Ⓓ Ⓔ
26 Ⓐ Ⓑ Ⓒ Ⓓ Ⓔ	26 Ⓐ Ⓑ Ⓒ Ⓓ Ⓔ	26 Ⓐ Ⓑ Ⓒ Ⓓ Ⓔ	26 Ⓐ Ⓑ Ⓒ Ⓓ Ⓔ	26 Ⓐ Ⓑ Ⓒ Ⓓ Ⓔ
27 Ⓐ Ⓑ Ⓒ Ⓓ Ⓔ	27 Ⓐ Ⓑ Ⓒ Ⓓ Ⓔ	27 Ⓐ Ⓑ Ⓒ Ⓓ Ⓔ	27 Ⓐ Ⓑ Ⓒ Ⓓ Ⓔ	27 Ⓐ Ⓑ Ⓒ Ⓓ Ⓔ
28 Ⓐ Ⓑ Ⓒ Ⓓ Ⓔ	28 Ⓐ Ⓑ Ⓒ Ⓓ Ⓔ	28 Ⓐ Ⓑ Ⓒ Ⓓ Ⓔ	28 Ⓐ Ⓑ Ⓒ Ⓓ Ⓔ	28 Ⓐ Ⓑ Ⓒ Ⓓ Ⓔ
29 Ⓐ Ⓑ Ⓒ Ⓓ Ⓔ	29 Ⓐ Ⓑ Ⓒ Ⓓ Ⓔ	29 Ⓐ Ⓑ Ⓒ Ⓓ Ⓔ	29 Ⓐ Ⓑ Ⓒ Ⓓ Ⓔ	29 Ⓐ Ⓑ Ⓒ Ⓓ Ⓔ
30 Ⓐ Ⓑ Ⓒ Ⓓ Ⓔ	30 Ⓐ Ⓑ Ⓒ Ⓓ Ⓔ	30 Ⓐ Ⓑ Ⓒ Ⓓ Ⓔ	30 Ⓐ Ⓑ Ⓒ Ⓓ Ⓔ	30 Ⓐ Ⓑ Ⓒ Ⓓ Ⓔ

14 PLEASE PRINT ALL INFORMATION

LAST NAME   FIRST

SOCIAL SECURITY/SOCIAL INSURANCE NO.

DATE OF BIRTH

MAILING ADDRESS

NOTE: If you have a new addre you must write LSAC at B 2000-C, Newtown, PA 18940 call 215.968.1001.

LR	LW	LCS

THE PREPTEST

SECTION I

Time—35 minutes

27 Questions

<u>Directions</u>: Each set of questions in this section is based on a single passage or a pair of passages. The questions are to be answered on the basis of what is <u>stated</u> or <u>implied</u> in the passage or pair of passages. For some of the questions, more than one of the choices could conceivably answer the question. However, you are to choose the <u>best</u> answer; that is, the response that most accurately and completely answers the question, and blacken the corresponding space on your answer sheet.

To study centuries-old earthquakes and the geologic faults that caused them, seismologists usually dig trenches along visible fault lines, looking for sediments that show evidence of having shifted. Using radiocarbon
(5) dating, they measure the quantity of the radioactive isotope carbon 14 present in wood or other organic material trapped in the sediments when they shifted. Since carbon 14 occurs naturally in organic materials and decays at a constant rate, the age of organic
(10) materials can be reconstructed from the amount of the isotope remaining in them. These data can show the location and frequency of past earthquakes and provide hints about the likelihood and location of future earthquakes.
(15) Geologists William Bull and Mark Brandon have recently developed a new method, called lichenometry, for detecting and dating past earthquakes. Bull and Brandon developed the method based on the fact that large earthquakes generate numerous simultaneous
(20) rockfalls in mountain ranges that are sensitive to seismic shaking. Instead of dating fault-line sediments, lichenometry involves measuring the size of lichens growing on the rocks exposed by these rockfalls. Lichens—symbiotic organisms consisting of a fungus
(25) and an alga—quickly colonize newly exposed rock surfaces in the wake of rockfalls, and once established they grow radially, flat against the rocks, at a slow but constant rate for as long as 1,000 years if left undisturbed. One species of North American lichen, for example,
(30) spreads outward by about 9.5 millimeters each century. Hence, the diameter of the largest lichen on a boulder provides direct evidence of when the boulder was dislodged and repositioned. If many rockfalls over a large geographic area occurred simultaneously, that
(35) pattern would imply that there had been a strong earthquake. The location of the earthquake's epicenter can then be determined by mapping these rockfalls, since they decrease in abundance as the distance from the epicenter increases.
(40) Lichenometry has distinct advantages over radiocarbon dating. Radiocarbon dating is accurate only to within plus or minus 40 years, because the amount of the carbon 14 isotope varies naturally in the environment depending on the intensity of the radiation
(45) striking Earth's upper atmosphere. Additionally, this intensity has fluctuated greatly during the past 300 years, causing many radiocarbon datings of events during this period to be of little value. Lichenometry, Bull and Brandon claim, can accurately date an
(50) earthquake to within ten years. They note, however, that using lichenometry requires careful site selection

and accurate calibration of lichen growth rates, adding that the method is best used for earthquakes that occurred within the last 500 years. Sites must be
(55) selected to minimize the influence of snow avalanches and other disturbances that would affect normal lichen growth, and conditions like shade and wind that promote faster lichen growth must be factored in.

1. Which one of the following most accurately expresses the main idea of the passage?

   (A) Lichenometry is a new method for dating past earthquakes that has advantages over radiocarbon dating.
   (B) Despite its limitations, lichenometry has been proven to be more accurate than any other method of discerning the dates of past earthquakes.
   (C) Most seismologists today have rejected radiocarbon dating and are embracing lichenometry as the most reliable method for studying past earthquakes.
   (D) Two geologists have revolutionized the study of past earthquakes by developing lichenometry, an easily applied method of earthquake detection and dating.
   (E) Radiocarbon dating, an unreliable test used in dating past earthquakes, can finally be abandoned now that lichenometry has been developed.

2. The passage provides information that most helps to answer which one of the following questions?

   (A) How do scientists measure lichen growth rates under the varying conditions that lichens may encounter?
   (B) How do scientists determine the intensity of the radiation striking Earth's upper atmosphere?
   (C) What are some of the conditions that encourage lichens to grow at a more rapid rate than usual?
   (D) What is the approximate date of the earliest earthquake that lichenometry has been used to identify?
   (E) What are some applications of the techniques involved in radiocarbon dating other than their use in studying past earthquakes?

GO ON TO THE NEXT PAGE.

3. What is the author's primary purpose in referring to the rate of growth of a North American lichen species (lines 29–30)?

   (A) to emphasize the rapidity with which lichen colonies can establish themselves on newly exposed rock surfaces
   (B) to offer an example of a lichen species with one of the slowest known rates of growth
   (C) to present additional evidence supporting the claim that environmental conditions can alter lichens' rate of growth
   (D) to explain why lichenometry works best for dating earthquakes that occurred in the last 500 years
   (E) to provide a sense of the sort of timescale on which lichen growth occurs

4. Which one of the following statements is most strongly supported by the passage?

   (A) Lichenometry is less accurate than radiocarbon dating in predicting the likelihood and location of future earthquakes.
   (B) Radiocarbon dating is unlikely to be helpful in dating past earthquakes that have no identifiable fault lines associated with them.
   (C) Radiocarbon dating and lichenometry are currently the only viable methods of detecting and dating past earthquakes.
   (D) Radiocarbon dating is more accurate than lichenometry in dating earthquakes that occurred approximately 400 years ago.
   (E) The usefulness of lichenometry for dating earthquakes is limited to geographic regions where factors that disturb or accelerate lichen growth generally do not occur.

5. The primary purpose of the first paragraph in relation to the rest of the passage is to describe

   (A) a well-known procedure that will then be examined on a step-by-step basis
   (B) an established procedure to which a new procedure will then be compared
   (C) an outdated procedure that will then be shown to be nonetheless useful in some situations
   (D) a traditional procedure that will then be contrasted with other traditional procedures
   (E) a popular procedure that will then be shown to have resulted in erroneous conclusions about a phenomenon

6. It can be inferred that the statements made by Bull and Brandon and reported in lines 50–58 rely on which one of the following assumptions?

   (A) While lichenometry is less accurate when it is used to date earthquakes that occurred more than 500 years ago, it is still more accurate than other methods for dating such earthquakes.
   (B) There is no reliable method for determining the intensity of the radiation now hitting Earth's upper atmosphere.
   (C) Lichens are able to grow only on the types of rocks that are common in mountainous regions.
   (D) The mountain ranges that produce the kinds of rockfalls studied in lichenometry are also subject to more frequent snowfalls and avalanches than other mountain ranges are.
   (E) The extent to which conditions like shade and wind have affected the growth of existing lichen colonies can be determined.

7. The passage indicates that using radiocarbon dating to date past earthquakes may be unreliable due to

   (A) the multiplicity of the types of organic matter that require analysis
   (B) the variable amount of organic materials caught in shifted sediments
   (C) the fact that fault lines related to past earthquakes are not always visible
   (D) the fluctuations in the amount of the carbon 14 isotope in the environment over time
   (E) the possibility that radiation has not always struck the upper atmosphere

8. Given the information in the passage, to which one of the following would lichenometry likely be most applicable?

   (A) identifying the number of times a particular river has flooded in the past 1,000 years
   (B) identifying the age of a fossilized skeleton of a mammal that lived many thousands of years ago
   (C) identifying the age of an ancient beach now underwater approximately 30 kilometers off the present shore
   (D) identifying the rate, in kilometers per century, at which a glacier has been receding up a mountain valley
   (E) identifying local trends in annual rainfall rates in a particular valley over the past five centuries

GO ON TO THE NEXT PAGE.

While courts have long allowed custom-made medical illustrations depicting personal injury to be presented as evidence in legal cases, the issue of whether they have a legitimate place in the courtroom
(5) is surrounded by ongoing debate and misinformation. Some opponents of their general use argue that while illustrations are sometimes invaluable in presenting the physical details of a personal injury, in all cases except those involving the most unusual injuries, illustrations
(10) from medical textbooks can be adequate. Most injuries, such as fractures and whiplash, they say, are rather generic in nature—certain commonly encountered forces act on particular areas of the body in standard ways—so they can be represented by
(15) generic illustrations.

Another line of complaint stems from the belief that custom-made illustrations often misrepresent the facts in order to comply with the partisan interests of litigants. Even some lawyers appear to share a version
(20) of this view, believing that such illustrations can be used to bolster a weak case. Illustrators are sometimes approached by lawyers who, unable to find medical experts to support their clients' claims, think that they can replace expert testimony with such deceptive
(25) professional illustrations. But this is mistaken. Even if an unscrupulous illustrator could be found, such illustrations would be inadmissible as evidence in the courtroom unless a medical expert were present to testify to their accuracy.
(30) It has also been maintained that custom-made illustrations may subtly distort the issues through the use of emphasis, coloration, and other means, even if they are technically accurate. But professional medical illustrators strive for objective accuracy and avoid
(35) devices that have inflammatory potential, sometimes even eschewing the use of color. Unlike illustrations in medical textbooks, which are designed to include the extensive detail required by medical students, custom-made medical illustrations are designed to
(40) include only the information that is relevant for those deciding a case. The end user is typically a jury or a judge, for whose benefit the depiction is reduced to the details that are crucial to determining the legally relevant facts. The more complex details often found
(45) in textbooks can be deleted so as not to confuse the issue. For example, illustrations of such things as veins and arteries would only get in the way when an illustration is supposed to be used to explain the nature of a bone fracture.
(50) Custom-made medical illustrations, which are based on a plaintiff's X rays, computerized tomography scans, and medical records and reports, are especially valuable in that they provide visual representations of data whose verbal description would
(55) be very complex. Expert testimony by medical professionals often relies heavily on the use of technical terminology, which those who are not specially trained in the field find difficult to translate mentally into visual imagery. Since, for most people,
(60) adequate understanding of physical data depends on thinking at least partly in visual terms, the clearly presented visual stimulation provided by custom-made illustrations can be quite instructive.

9. Which one of the following is most analogous to the role that, according to the author, custom-made medical illustrations play in personal injury cases?

(A) schematic drawings accompanying an engineer's oral presentation
(B) road maps used by people unfamiliar with an area so that they will not have to get verbal instructions from strangers
(C) children's drawings that psychologists use to detect wishes and anxieties not apparent in the children's behavior
(D) a reproduction of a famous painting in an art history textbook
(E) an artist's preliminary sketches for a painting

10. Based on the passage, which one of the following is the author most likely to believe about illustrations in medical textbooks?

(A) They tend to rely less on the use of color than do custom-made medical illustrations.
(B) They are inadmissible in a courtroom unless a medical expert is present to testify to their accuracy.
(C) They are in many cases drawn by the same individuals who draw custom-made medical illustrations for courtroom use.
(D) They are believed by most lawyers to be less prone than custom-made medical illustrations to misrepresent the nature of a personal injury.
(E) In many cases they are more apt to confuse jurors than are custom-made medical illustrations.

11. The passage states that a role of medical experts in relation to custom-made medical illustrations in the courtroom is to

(A) decide which custom-made medical illustrations should be admissible
(B) temper the impact of the illustrations on judges and jurors who are not medical professionals
(C) make medical illustrations understandable to judges and jurors
(D) provide opinions to attorneys as to which illustrations, if any, would be useful
(E) provide their opinions as to the accuracy of the illustrations

GO ON TO THE NEXT PAGE.

12. According to the passage, one of the ways that medical textbook illustrations differ from custom-made medical illustrations is that

(A) custom-made medical illustrations accurately represent human anatomy, whereas medical textbook illustrations do not

(B) medical textbook illustrations employ color freely, whereas custom-made medical illustrations must avoid color

(C) medical textbook illustrations are objective, while custom-made medical illustrations are subjective

(D) medical textbook illustrations are very detailed, whereas custom-made medical illustrations include only details that are relevant to the case

(E) medical textbook illustrations are readily comprehended by nonmedical audiences, whereas custom-made medical illustrations are not

13. The author's attitude toward the testimony of medical experts in personal injury cases is most accurately described as

(A) appreciation of the difficulty involved in explaining medical data to judges and jurors together with skepticism concerning the effectiveness of such testimony

(B) admiration for the experts' technical knowledge coupled with disdain for the communications skills of medical professionals

(C) acceptance of the accuracy of such testimony accompanied with awareness of the limitations of a presentation that is entirely verbal

(D) respect for the medical profession tempered by apprehension concerning the tendency of medical professionals to try to overwhelm judges and jurors with technical details

(E) respect for expert witnesses combined with intolerance of the use of technical terminology

14. The author's primary purpose in the third paragraph is to

(A) argue for a greater use of custom-made medical illustrations in court cases involving personal injury

(B) reply to a variant of the objection to custom-made medical illustrations raised in the second paragraph

(C) argue against the position that illustrations from medical textbooks are well suited for use in the courtroom

(D) discuss in greater detail why custom-made medical illustrations are controversial

(E) describe the differences between custom-made medical illustrations and illustrations from medical textbooks

GO ON TO THE NEXT PAGE.

Passage A

Because dental caries (decay) is strongly linked to consumption of the sticky, carbohydrate-rich staples of agricultural diets, prehistoric human teeth can provide clues about when a population made the transition
(5) from a hunter-gatherer diet to an agricultural one. Caries formation is influenced by several factors, including tooth structure, bacteria in the mouth, and diet. In particular, caries formation is affected by carbohydrates' texture and composition, since
(10) carbohydrates more readily stick to teeth.

Many researchers have demonstrated the link between carbohydrate consumption and caries. In North America, Leigh studied caries in archaeologically derived teeth, noting that caries rates differed between
(15) indigenous populations that primarily consumed meat (a Sioux sample showed almost no caries) and those heavily dependent on cultivated maize (a Zuni sample had 75 percent carious teeth). Leigh's findings have been frequently confirmed by other researchers, who
(20) have shown that, in general, the greater a population's dependence on agriculture is, the higher its rate of caries formation will be.

Under some circumstances, however, nonagricultural populations may exhibit relatively
(25) high caries rates. For example, early nonagricultural populations in western North America who consumed large amounts of highly processed stone-ground flour made from gathered acorns show relatively high caries frequencies. And wild plants collected by the Hopi
(30) included several species with high cariogenic potential, notably pinyon nuts and wild tubers.

Passage B

Archaeologists recovered human skeletal remains interred over a 2,000-year period in prehistoric Ban Chiang, Thailand. The site's early inhabitants
(35) appear to have had a hunter-gatherer-cultivator economy. Evidence indicates that, over time, the population became increasingly dependent on agriculture.

Research suggests that agricultural intensification
(40) results in declining human health, including dental health. Studies show that dental caries is uncommon in pre-agricultural populations. Increased caries frequency may result from increased consumption of starchy-sticky foodstuffs or from alterations in tooth wear. The
(45) wearing down of tooth crown surfaces reduces caries formation by removing fissures that can trap food particles. A reduction of fiber or grit in a diet may diminish tooth wear, thus increasing caries frequency. However, severe wear that exposes a tooth's pulp
(50) cavity may also result in caries.

The diet of Ban Chiang's inhabitants included some cultivated rice and yams from the beginning of the period represented by the recovered remains. These were part of a varied diet that also included
(55) wild plant and animal foods. Since both rice and yams are carbohydrates, increased reliance on either or both should theoretically result in increased caries frequency.

Yet comparisons of caries frequency in the Early and Late Ban Chiang Groups indicate that overall
(60) caries frequency is slightly greater in the Early Group. Tooth wear patterns do not indicate tooth wear changes between Early and Late Groups that would explain this unexpected finding. It is more likely that, although dependence on agriculture increased, the diet
(65) in the Late period remained varied enough that no single food dominated. Furthermore, there may have been a shift from sweeter carbohydrates (yams) toward rice, a less cariogenic carbohydrate.

15. Both passages are primarily concerned with examining which one of the following topics?

(A) evidence of the development of agriculture in the archaeological record

(B) the impact of agriculture on the overall health of human populations

(C) the effects of carbohydrate-rich foods on caries formation in strictly agricultural societies

(D) the archaeological evidence regarding when the first agricultural society arose

(E) the extent to which pre-agricultural populations were able to obtain carbohydrate-rich foods

16. Which one of the following distinguishes the Ban Chiang populations discussed in passage B from the populations discussed in the last paragraph of passage A?

(A) While the Ban Chiang populations consumed several highly cariogenic foods, the populations discussed in the last paragraph of passage A did not.

(B) While the Ban Chiang populations ate cultivated foods, the populations discussed in the last paragraph of passage A did not.

(C) While the Ban Chiang populations consumed a diet consisting primarily of carbohydrates, the populations discussed in the last paragraph of passage A did not.

(D) While the Ban Chiang populations exhibited very high levels of tooth wear, the populations discussed in the last paragraph of passage A did not.

(E) While the Ban Chiang populations ate certain highly processed foods, the populations discussed in the last paragraph of passage A did not.

GO ON TO THE NEXT PAGE.

17. Passage B most strongly supports which one of the following statements about fiber and grit in a diet?

   (A) They can either limit or promote caries formation, depending on their prevalence in the diet.
   (B) They are typically consumed in greater quantities as a population adopts agriculture.
   (C) They have a negative effect on overall health since they have no nutritional value.
   (D) They contribute to the formation of fissures in tooth surfaces.
   (E) They increase the stickiness of carbohydrate-rich foods.

18. Which one of the following is mentioned in both passages as evidence tending to support the prevailing view regarding the relationship between dental caries and carbohydrate consumption?

   (A) the effect of consuming highly processed foods on caries formation
   (B) the relatively low incidence of caries among nonagricultural people
   (C) the effect of fiber and grit in the diet on caries formation
   (D) the effect of the consumption of wild foods on tooth wear
   (E) the effect of agricultural intensification on overall human health

19. It is most likely that both authors would agree with which one of the following statements about dental caries?

   (A) The incidence of dental caries increases predictably in populations over time.
   (B) Dental caries is often difficult to detect in teeth recovered from archaeological sites.
   (C) Dental caries tends to be more prevalent in populations with a hunter-gatherer diet than in populations with an agricultural diet.
   (D) The frequency of dental caries in a population does not necessarily correspond directly to the population's degree of dependence on agriculture.
   (E) The formation of dental caries tends to be more strongly linked to tooth wear than to the consumption of a particular kind of food.

20. Each passage suggests which one of the following about carbohydrate-rich foods?

   (A) Varieties that are cultivated have a greater tendency to cause caries than varieties that grow wild.
   (B) Those that require substantial processing do not play a role in hunter-gatherer diets.
   (C) Some of them naturally have a greater tendency than others to cause caries.
   (D) Some of them reduce caries formation because their relatively high fiber content increases tooth wear.
   (E) The cariogenic potential of a given variety increases if it is cultivated rather than gathered in the wild.

21. The evidence from Ban Chiang discussed in passage B relates to the generalization reported in the second paragraph of passage A (lines 20–22) in which one of the following ways?

   (A) The evidence confirms the generalization.
   (B) The evidence tends to support the generalization.
   (C) The evidence is irrelevant to the generalization.
   (D) The evidence does not conform to the generalization.
   (E) The evidence disproves the generalization.

GO ON TO THE NEXT PAGE.

Recent criticism has sought to align Sarah Orne Jewett, a notable writer of regional fiction in the nineteenth-century United States, with the domestic novelists of the previous generation. Her work does
(5) resemble the domestic novels of the 1850s in its focus on women, their domestic occupations, and their social interactions, with men relegated to the periphery. But it also differs markedly from these antecedents. The world depicted in the latter revolves around children.
(10) Young children play prominent roles in the domestic novels and the work of child rearing—the struggle to instill a mother's values in a child's character—is their chief source of drama. By contrast, children and child rearing are almost entirely absent from the world of
(15) Jewett's fiction. Even more strikingly, while the literary world of the earlier domestic novelists is insistently religious, grounded in the structures of Protestant religious belief, to turn from these writers to Jewett is to encounter an almost wholly secular world.

(20) To the extent that these differences do not merely reflect the personal preferences of the authors, we might attribute them to such historical transformations as the migration of the rural young to cities or the increasing secularization of society. But while such
(25) factors may help to explain the differences, it can be argued that these differences ultimately reflect different conceptions of the nature and purpose of fiction. The domestic novel of the mid-nineteenth century is based on a conception of fiction as part of
(30) a continuum that also included writings devoted to piety and domestic instruction, bound together by a common goal of promoting domestic morality and religious belief. It was not uncommon for the same multipurpose book to be indistinguishably a novel, a
(35) child-rearing manual, and a tract on Christian duty. The more didactic aims are absent from Jewett's writing, which rather embodies the late nineteenth-century "high-cultural" conception of fiction as an autonomous sphere with value in and of itself.

(40) This high-cultural aesthetic was one among several conceptions of fiction operative in the United States in the 1850s and 1860s, but it became the dominant one later in the nineteenth century and remained so for most of the twentieth. On this
(45) conception, fiction came to be seen as pure art: a work was to be viewed in isolation and valued for the formal arrangement of its elements rather than for its larger social connections or the promotion of extraliterary goods. Thus, unlike the domestic novelists, Jewett
(50) intended her works not as a means to an end but as an end in themselves. This fundamental difference should be given more weight in assessing their affinities than any superficial similarity in subject matter.

22. The passage most helps to answer which one of the following questions?

(A) Did any men write domestic novels in the 1850s?
(B) Were any widely read domestic novels written after the 1860s?
(C) How did migration to urban areas affect the development of domestic fiction in the 1850s?
(D) What is an effect that Jewett's conception of literary art had on her fiction?
(E) With what region of the United States were at least some of Jewett's writings concerned?

23. It can be inferred from the passage that the author would be most likely to view the "recent criticism" mentioned in line 1 as

(A) advocating a position that is essentially correct even though some powerful arguments can be made against it
(B) making a true claim about Jewett, but for the wrong reasons
(C) making a claim that is based on some reasonable evidence and is initially plausible but ultimately mistaken
(D) questionable, because it relies on a currently dominant literary aesthetic that takes too narrow a view of the proper goals of fiction
(E) based on speculation for which there is no reasonable support, and therefore worthy of dismissal

24. In saying that domestic fiction was based on a conception of fiction as part of a "continuum" (line 30), the author most likely means which one of the following?

(A) Domestic fiction was part of an ongoing tradition stretching back into the past.
(B) Fiction was not treated as clearly distinct from other categories of writing.
(C) Domestic fiction was often published in serial form.
(D) Fiction is constantly evolving.
(E) Domestic fiction promoted the cohesiveness and hence the continuity of society.

GO ON TO THE NEXT PAGE.

25. Which one of the following most accurately states the primary function of the passage?

   (A) It proposes and defends a radical redefinition of several historical categories of literary style.
   (B) It proposes an evaluation of a particular style of writing, of which one writer's work is cited as a paradigmatic case.
   (C) It argues for a reappraisal of a set of long-held assumptions about the historical connections among a group of writers.
   (D) It weighs the merits of two opposing conceptions of the nature of fiction.
   (E) It rejects a way of classifying a particular writer's work and defends an alternative view.

26. Which one of the following most accurately represents the structure of the second paragraph?

   (A) The author considers and rejects a number of possible explanations for a phenomenon, concluding that any attempt at explanation does violence to the unity of the phenomenon.
   (B) The author shows that two explanatory hypotheses are incompatible with each other and gives reasons for preferring one of them.
   (C) The author describes several explanatory hypotheses and argues that they are not really distinct from one another.
   (D) The author proposes two versions of a classificatory hypothesis, indicates the need for some such hypothesis, and then sets out a counterargument in preparation for rejecting that counterargument in the following paragraph.
   (E) The author mentions a number of explanatory hypotheses, gives a mildly favorable comment on them, and then advocates and elaborates another explanation that the author considers to be more fundamental.

27. The differing conceptions of fiction held by Jewett and the domestic novelists can most reasonably be taken as providing an answer to which one of the following questions?

   (A) Why was Jewett unwilling to feature children and religious themes as prominently in her works as the domestic novelists featured them in theirs?
   (B) Why did both Jewett and the domestic novelists focus primarily on rural as opposed to urban concerns?
   (C) Why was Jewett not constrained to feature children and religion as prominently in her works as domestic novelists were?
   (D) Why did both Jewett and the domestic novelists focus predominantly on women and their concerns?
   (E) Why was Jewett unable to feature children or religion as prominently in her works as the domestic novelists featured them in theirs?

S T O P

IF YOU FINISH BEFORE TIME IS CALLED, YOU MAY CHECK YOUR WORK ON THIS SECTION ONLY.
DO NOT WORK ON ANY OTHER SECTION IN THE TEST.

SECTION II

Time—35 minutes

26 Questions

Directions: The questions in this section are based on the reasoning contained in brief statements or passages. For some questions, more than one of the choices could conceivably answer the question. However, you are to choose the best answer; that is, the response that most accurately and completely answers the question. You should not make assumptions that are by commonsense standards implausible, superfluous, or incompatible with the passage. After you have chosen the best answer, blacken the corresponding space on your answer sheet.

1. In a recent study, a group of young children were taught the word "stairs" while walking up and down a flight of stairs. Later that day, when the children were shown a video of a person climbing a ladder, they all called the ladder stairs.

    Which one of the following principles is best illustrated by the study described above?

    (A)   When young children repeatedly hear a word without seeing the object denoted by the word, they sometimes apply the word to objects not denoted by the word.
    (B)   Young children best learn words when they are shown how the object denoted by the word is used.
    (C)   The earlier in life a child encounters and uses an object, the easier it is for that child to learn how not to misuse the word denoting that object.
    (D)   Young children who learn a word by observing how the object denoted by that word is used sometimes apply that word to a different object that is similarly used.
    (E)   Young children best learn the names of objects when the objects are present at the time the children learn the words and when no other objects are simultaneously present.

2. Among people who live to the age of 100 or more, a large proportion have led "unhealthy" lives: smoking, consuming alcohol, eating fatty foods, and getting little exercise. Since such behavior often leads to shortened life spans, it is likely that exceptionally long-lived people are genetically disposed to having long lives.

    Which one of the following, if true, most strengthens the argument?

    (A)   There is some evidence that consuming a moderate amount of alcohol can counteract the effects of eating fatty foods.
    (B)   Some of the exceptionally long-lived people who do not smoke or drink do eat fatty foods and get little exercise.
    (C)   Some of the exceptionally long-lived people who exercise regularly and avoid fatty foods do smoke or consume alcohol.
    (D)   Some people who do not live to the age of 100 also lead unhealthy lives.
    (E)   Nearly all people who live to 100 or more have siblings who are also long-lived.

3. Medications with an unpleasant taste are generally produced only in tablet, capsule, or soft-gel form. The active ingredient in medication M is a waxy substance that cannot tolerate the heat used to manufacture tablets because it has a low melting point. So, since the company developing M does not have soft-gel manufacturing technology and manufactures all its medications itself, M will most likely be produced in capsule form.

    The conclusion is most strongly supported by the reasoning in the argument if which one of the following is assumed?

    (A)   Medication M can be produced in liquid form.
    (B)   Medication M has an unpleasant taste.
    (C)   No medication is produced in both capsule and soft-gel form.
    (D)   Most medications with a low melting point are produced in soft-gel form.
    (E)   Medications in capsule form taste less unpleasant than those in tablet or soft-gel form.

GO ON TO THE NEXT PAGE.

4. Carol Morris wants to own a majority of the shares of the city's largest newspaper, *The Daily*. The only obstacle to Morris's amassing a majority of these shares is that Azedcorp, which currently owns a majority, has steadfastly refused to sell. Industry analysts nevertheless predict that Morris will soon be the majority owner of *The Daily*.

Which one of the following, if true, provides the most support for the industry analysts' prediction?

(A) Azedcorp does not own shares of any newspaper other than *The Daily*.

(B) Morris has recently offered Azedcorp much more for its shares of *The Daily* than Azedcorp paid for them.

(C) No one other than Morris has expressed any interest in purchasing a majority of *The Daily*'s shares.

(D) Morris already owns more shares of *The Daily* than anyone except Azedcorp.

(E) Azedcorp is financially so weak that bankruptcy will probably soon force the sale of its newspaper holdings.

5. Area resident: Childhood lead poisoning has declined steadily since the 1970s, when leaded gasoline was phased out and lead paint was banned. But recent statistics indicate that 25 percent of this area's homes still contain lead paint that poses significant health hazards. Therefore, if we eliminate the lead paint in those homes, childhood lead poisoning in the area will finally be eradicated.

The area resident's argument is flawed in that it

(A) relies on statistical claims that are likely to be unreliable

(B) relies on an assumption that is tantamount to assuming that the conclusion is true

(C) fails to consider that there may be other significant sources of lead in the area's environment

(D) takes for granted that lead paint in homes can be eliminated economically

(E) takes for granted that children reside in all of the homes in the area that contain lead paint

6. Although some nutritional facts about soft drinks are listed on their labels, exact caffeine content is not. Listing exact caffeine content would make it easier to limit, but not eliminate, one's caffeine intake. If it became easier for people to limit, but not eliminate, their caffeine intake, many people would do so, which would improve their health.

If all the statements above are true, which one of the following must be true?

(A) The health of at least some people would improve if exact caffeine content were listed on soft-drink labels.

(B) Many people will be unable to limit their caffeine intake if exact caffeine content is not listed on soft-drink labels.

(C) Many people will find it difficult to eliminate their caffeine intake if they have to guess exactly how much caffeine is in their soft drinks.

(D) People who wish to eliminate, rather than simply limit, their caffeine intake would benefit if exact caffeine content were listed on soft-drink labels.

(E) The health of at least some people would worsen if everyone knew exactly how much caffeine was in their soft drinks.

7. When the famous art collector Vidmar died, a public auction of her collection, the largest privately owned, was held. "I can't possibly afford any of those works because hers is among the most valuable collections ever assembled by a single person," declared art lover MacNeil.

The flawed pattern of reasoning in which one of the following is most closely parallel to that in MacNeil's argument?

(A) Each word in the book is in French. So the whole book is in French.

(B) The city council voted unanimously to adopt the plan. So councilperson Martinez voted to adopt the plan.

(C) This paragraph is long. So the sentences that comprise it are long.

(D) The members of the company are old. So the company itself is old.

(E) The atoms comprising this molecule are elements. So the molecule itself is an element.

GO ON TO THE NEXT PAGE.

8. A leading critic of space exploration contends that it would be wrong, given current technology, to send a group of explorers to Mars, since the explorers would be unlikely to survive the trip. But that exaggerates the risk. There would be a well-engineered backup system at every stage of the long and complicated journey. A fatal catastrophe is quite unlikely at any given stage if such a backup system is in place.

The reasoning in the argument is flawed in that the argument

(A) infers that something is true of a whole merely from the fact that it is true of each of the parts

(B) infers that something cannot occur merely from the fact that it is unlikely to occur

(C) draws a conclusion about what must be the case based on evidence about what is probably the case

(D) infers that something will work merely because it could work

(E) rejects a view merely on the grounds that an inadequate argument has been made for it

9. A retrospective study is a scientific study that tries to determine the causes of subjects' present characteristics by looking for significant connections between the present characteristics of subjects and what happened to those subjects in the past, before the study began. Because retrospective studies of human subjects must use the subjects' reports about their own pasts, however, such studies cannot reliably determine the causes of human subjects' present characteristics.

Which one of the following, if assumed, enables the argument's conclusion to be properly drawn?

(A) Whether or not a study of human subjects can reliably determine the causes of those subjects' present characteristics may depend at least in part on the extent to which that study uses inaccurate reports about the subjects' pasts.

(B) A retrospective study cannot reliably determine the causes of human subjects' present characteristics unless there exist correlations between the present characteristics of the subjects and what happened to those subjects in the past.

(C) In studies of human subjects that attempt to find connections between subjects' present characteristics and what happened to those subjects in the past, the subjects' reports about their own pasts are highly susceptible to inaccuracy.

(D) If a study of human subjects uses only accurate reports about the subjects' pasts, then that study can reliably determine the causes of those subjects' present characteristics.

(E) Every scientific study in which researchers look for significant connections between the present characteristics of subjects and what happened to those subjects in the past must use the subjects' reports about their own pasts.

GO ON TO THE NEXT PAGE.

10. Gigantic passenger planes currently being developed will have enough space to hold shops and lounges in addition to passenger seating. However, the additional space will more likely be used for more passenger seating. The number of passengers flying the air-traffic system is expected to triple within 20 years, and it will be impossible for airports to accommodate enough normal-sized jet planes to carry that many passengers.

Which one of the following most accurately states the conclusion drawn in the argument?

(A)   Gigantic planes currently being developed will have enough space in them to hold shops and lounges as well as passenger seating.
(B)   The additional space in the gigantic planes currently being developed is more likely to be filled with passenger seating than with shops and lounges.
(C)   The number of passengers flying the air-traffic system is expected to triple within 20 years.
(D)   In 20 years, it will be impossible for airports to accommodate enough normal-sized planes to carry the number of passengers that are expected to be flying then.
(E)   In 20 years, most airline passengers will be flying in gigantic passenger planes.

11. Scientist: To study the comparative effectiveness of two experimental medications for athlete's foot, a representative sample of people with athlete's foot were randomly assigned to one of two groups. One group received only medication M, and the other received only medication N. The only people whose athlete's foot was cured had been given medication M.

Reporter: This means, then, that if anyone in the study had athlete's foot that was not cured, that person did not receive medication M.

Which one of the following most accurately describes the reporter's error in reasoning?

(A)   The reporter concludes from evidence showing only that M can cure athlete's foot that M always cures athlete's foot.
(B)   The reporter illicitly draws a conclusion about the population as a whole on the basis of a study conducted only on a sample of the population.
(C)   The reporter presumes, without providing justification, that medications M and N are available to people who have athlete's foot but did not participate in the study.
(D)   The reporter fails to allow for the possibility that athlete's foot may be cured even if neither of the two medications studied is taken.
(E)   The reporter presumes, without providing justification, that there is no sizeable subgroup of people whose athlete's foot will be cured only if they do not take medication M.

12. Paleontologist: Plesiosauromorphs were gigantic, long-necked marine reptiles that ruled the oceans during the age of the dinosaurs. Most experts believe that plesiosauromorphs lurked and quickly ambushed their prey. However, plesiosauromorphs probably hunted by chasing their prey over long distances. Plesiosauromorph fins were quite long and thin, like the wings of birds specialized for long-distance flight.

Which one of the following is an assumption on which the paleontologist's argument depends?

(A)   Birds and reptiles share many physical features because they descend from common evolutionary ancestors.
(B)   During the age of dinosaurs, plesiosauromorphs were the only marine reptiles that had long, thin fins.
(C)   A gigantic marine animal would not be able to find enough food to meet the caloric requirements dictated by its body size if it did not hunt by chasing prey over long distances.
(D)   Most marine animals that chase prey over long distances are specialized for long-distance swimming.
(E)   The shape of a marine animal's fin affects the way the animal swims in the same way as the shape of a bird's wing affects the way the bird flies.

13. Buying elaborate screensavers—programs that put moving images on a computer monitor to prevent damage—can cost a company far more in employee time than it saves in electricity and monitor protection. Employees cannot resist spending time playing with screensavers that flash interesting graphics across their screens.

Which one of the following most closely conforms to the principle illustrated above?

(A)   A school that chooses textbooks based on student preference may not get the most economical package.
(B)   An energy-efficient insulation system may cost more up front but will ultimately save money over the life of the house.
(C)   The time that it takes to have a pizza delivered may be longer than it takes to cook a complete dinner.
(D)   A complicated hotel security system may cost more in customer goodwill than it saves in losses by theft.
(E)   An electronic keyboard may be cheaper to buy than a piano but more expensive to repair.

GO ON TO THE NEXT PAGE.

14. Music professor: Because rap musicians can work alone in a recording studio, they need not accommodate supporting musicians' wishes. Further, learning to rap is not as formal a process as learning an instrument. Thus, rap is an extremely individualistic and nontraditional musical form.

Music critic: But rap appeals to tradition by using bits of older songs. Besides, the themes and styles of rap have developed into a tradition. And successful rap musicians do not perform purely idiosyncratically but conform their work to the preferences of the public.

The music critic's response to the music professor's argument

(A) challenges it by offering evidence against one of the stated premises on which its conclusion concerning rap music is based

(B) challenges its conclusion concerning rap music by offering certain additional observations that the music professor does not take into account in his argument

(C) challenges the grounds on which the music professor generalizes from the particular context of rap music to the broader context of musical tradition and individuality

(D) challenges it by offering an alternative explanation of phenomena that the music professor cites as evidence for his thesis about rap music

(E) challenges each of a group of claims about tradition and individuality in music that the music professor gives as evidence in his argument

15. Speaker: Like many contemporary critics, Smith argues that the true meaning of an author's statements can be understood only through insight into the author's social circumstances. But this same line of analysis can be applied to Smith's own words. Thus, if she is right we should be able, at least in part, to discern from Smith's social circumstances the "true meaning" of Smith's statements. This, in turn, suggests that Smith herself is not aware of the true meaning of her own words.

The speaker's main conclusion logically follows if which one of the following is assumed?

(A) Insight into the intended meaning of an author's work is not as important as insight into its true meaning.

(B) Smith lacks insight into her own social circumstances.

(C) There is just one meaning that Smith intends her work to have.

(D) Smith's theory about the relation of social circumstances to the understanding of meaning lacks insight.

(E) The intended meaning of an author's work is not always good evidence of its true meaning.

16. Tissue biopsies taken on patients who have undergone throat surgery show that those who snored frequently were significantly more likely to have serious abnormalities in their throat muscles than those who snored rarely or not at all. This shows that snoring can damage the throat of the snorer.

Which one of the following, if true, most strengthens the argument?

(A) The study relied on the subjects' self-reporting to determine whether or not they snored frequently.

(B) The patients' throat surgery was not undertaken to treat abnormalities in their throat muscles.

(C) All of the test subjects were of similar age and weight and in similar states of health.

(D) People who have undergone throat surgery are no more likely to snore than people who have not undergone throat surgery.

(E) The abnormalities in the throat muscles discovered in the study do not cause snoring.

GO ON TO THE NEXT PAGE.

17. One should never sacrifice one's health in order to acquire money, for without health, happiness is not obtainable.

The conclusion of the argument follows logically if which one of the following is assumed?

(A) Money should be acquired only if its acquisition will not make happiness unobtainable.

(B) In order to be happy one must have either money or health.

(C) Health should be valued only as a precondition for happiness.

(D) Being wealthy is, under certain conditions, conducive to unhappiness.

(E) Health is more conducive to happiness than wealth is.

18. Vanessa: All computer code must be written by a pair of programmers working at a single workstation. This is needed to prevent programmers from writing idiosyncratic code that can be understood only by the original programmer.

Jo: Most programming projects are kept afloat by the best programmers on the team, who are typically at least 100 times more productive than the worst. Since they generally work best when they work alone, the most productive programmers must be allowed to work by themselves.

Each of the following assignments of computer programmers is consistent both with the principle expressed by Vanessa and with the principle expressed by Jo EXCEPT:

(A) Olga and Kensuke are both programmers of roughly average productivity who feel that they are more productive when working alone. They have been assigned to work together at a single workstation.

(B) John is experienced but is not among the most productive programmers on the team. He has been assigned to mentor Tyrone, a new programmer who is not yet very productive. They are to work together at a single workstation.

(C) Although not among the most productive programmers on the team, Chris is more productive than Jennifer. They have been assigned to work together at a single workstation.

(D) Yolanda is the most productive programmer on the team. She has been assigned to work with Mike, who is also very productive. They are to work together at the same workstation.

(E) Kevin and Amy both have a reputation for writing idiosyncratic code; neither is unusually productive. They have been assigned to work together at the same workstation.

19. In West Calverton, most pet stores sell exotic birds, and most of those that sell exotic birds also sell tropical fish. However, any pet store there that sells tropical fish but not exotic birds does sell gerbils; and no independently owned pet stores in West Calverton sell gerbils.

If the statements above are true, which one of the following must be true?

(A) Most pet stores in West Calverton that are not independently owned do not sell exotic birds.

(B) No pet stores in West Calverton that sell tropical fish and exotic birds sell gerbils.

(C) Some pet stores in West Calverton that sell gerbils also sell exotic birds.

(D) No independently owned pet store in West Calverton sells tropical fish but not exotic birds.

(E) Any independently owned pet store in West Calverton that does not sell tropical fish sells exotic birds.

20. Astronomer: Earlier estimates of the distances of certain stars from Earth would mean that these stars are about 1 billion years older than the universe itself, an impossible scenario. My estimates of the distances indicate that these stars are much farther away than previously thought. And the farther away the stars are, the greater their intrinsic brightness must be, given their appearance to us on Earth. So the new estimates of these stars' distances from Earth help resolve the earlier conflict between the ages of these stars and the age of the universe.

Which one of the following, if true, most helps to explain why the astronomer's estimates of the stars' distances from Earth help resolve the earlier conflict between the ages of these stars and the age of the universe?

(A) The stars are the oldest objects yet discovered in the universe.

(B) The younger the universe is, the more bright stars it is likely to have.

(C) The brighter a star is, the younger it is.

(D) How bright celestial objects appear to be depends on how far away from the observer they are.

(E) New telescopes allow astronomers to see a greater number of distant stars.

GO ON TO THE NEXT PAGE.

21. Most large nurseries sell raspberry plants primarily to commercial raspberry growers and sell only plants that are guaranteed to be disease-free. However, the shipment of raspberry plants that Johnson received from Wally's Plants carried a virus that commonly afflicts raspberries.

Which one of the following is most strongly supported by the information above?

(A) If Johnson is a commercial raspberry grower and Wally's Plants is not a large nursery, then the shipment of raspberry plants that Johnson received was probably guaranteed to be disease-free.

(B) Johnson is probably not a commercial raspberry grower if the shipment of raspberry plants that Johnson received from Wally's Plants was not entirely as it was guaranteed to be.

(C) If Johnson is not a commercial raspberry grower, then Wally's Plants is probably not a large nursery.

(D) Wally's Plants is probably not a large, well-run nursery if it sells its raspberry plants primarily to commercial raspberry growers.

(E) If Wally's Plants is a large nursery, then the raspberry plants that Johnson received in the shipment were probably not entirely as they were guaranteed to be.

22. Drug company manager: Our newest product is just not selling. One way to save it would be a new marketing campaign. This would not guarantee success, but it is one chance to save the product, so we should try it.

Which one of the following, if true, most seriously weakens the manager's argument?

(A) The drug company has invested heavily in its newest product, and losses due to this product would be harmful to the company's profits.

(B) Many new products fail whether or not they are supported by marketing campaigns.

(C) The drug company should not undertake a new marketing campaign for its newest product if the campaign has no chance to succeed.

(D) Undertaking a new marketing campaign would endanger the drug company's overall position by necessitating cutbacks in existing marketing campaigns.

(E) Consumer demand for the drug company's other products has been strong in the time since the company's newest product was introduced.

23. Consumer advocate: TMD, a pesticide used on peaches, shows no effects on human health when it is ingested in the amount present in the per capita peach consumption in this country. But while 80 percent of the population eat no peaches, others, including small children, consume much more than the national average, and thus ingest disproportionately large amounts of TMD. So even though the use of TMD on peaches poses minimal risk to most of the population, it has not been shown to be an acceptable practice.

Which one of the following principles, if valid, most helps to justify the consumer advocate's argumentation?

(A) The possibility that more data about a pesticide's health effects might reveal previously unknown risks at low doses warrants caution in assessing that pesticide's overall risks.

(B) The consequences of using a pesticide are unlikely to be acceptable when a majority of the population is likely to ingest it.

(C) Use of a pesticide is acceptable only if it is used for its intended purpose and the pesticide has been shown not to harm any portion of the population.

(D) Society has a special obligation to protect small children from pesticides unless average doses received by the population are low and have not been shown to be harmful to children's health.

(E) Measures taken to protect the population from a harm sometimes turn out to be the cause of a more serious harm to certain segments of the population.

24. Legal commentator: The goal of a recently enacted law that bans smoking in workplaces is to protect employees from secondhand smoke. But the law is written in such a way that it cannot be interpreted as ever prohibiting people from smoking in their own homes.

The statements above, if true, provide a basis for rejecting which one of the following claims?

(A) The law will be interpreted in a way that is inconsistent with the intentions of the legislators who supported it.

(B) Supporters of the law believe that it will have a significant impact on the health of many workers.

(C) The law offers no protection from secondhand smoke for people outside of their workplaces.

(D) Most people believe that smokers have a fundamental right to smoke in their own homes.

(E) The law will protect domestic workers such as housecleaners from secondhand smoke in their workplaces.

GO ON TO THE NEXT PAGE.

25. University president: Our pool of applicants has been shrinking over the past few years. One possible explanation of this unwelcome phenomenon is that we charge too little for tuition and fees. Prospective students and their parents conclude that the quality of education they would receive at this institution is not as high as that offered by institutions with higher tuition. So, if we want to increase the size of our applicant pool, we need to raise our tuition and fees.

The university president's argument requires the assumption that

(A) the proposed explanation for the decline in applications applies in this case
(B) the quality of a university education is dependent on the amount of tuition charged by the university
(C) an increase in tuition and fees at the university would guarantee a larger applicant pool
(D) there is no additional explanation for the university's shrinking applicant pool
(E) the amount charged by the university for tuition has not increased in recent years

26. Editorial: It has been suggested that private, for-profit companies should be hired to supply clean drinking water to areas of the world where it is unavailable now. But water should not be supplied by private companies. After all, clean water is essential for human health, and the purpose of a private company is to produce profit, not to promote health.

Which one of the following principles, if valid, would most help to justify the reasoning in the editorial?

(A) A private company should not be allowed to supply a commodity that is essential to human health unless that commodity is also supplied by a government agency.
(B) If something is essential for human health and private companies are unwilling or unable to supply it, then it should be supplied by a government agency.
(C) Drinking water should never be supplied by an organization that is not able to consistently supply clean, safe water.
(D) The mere fact that something actually promotes human health is not sufficient to show that its purpose is to promote health.
(E) If something is necessary for human health, then it should be provided by an organization whose primary purpose is the promotion of health.

S T O P

IF YOU FINISH BEFORE TIME IS CALLED, YOU MAY CHECK YOUR WORK ON THIS SECTION ONLY.
DO NOT WORK ON ANY OTHER SECTION IN THE TEST.

SECTION III
Time—35 minutes
23 Questions

Directions: Each group of questions in this section is based on a set of conditions. In answering some of the questions, it may be useful to draw a rough diagram. Choose the response that most accurately and completely answers each question and blacken the corresponding space on your answer sheet.

Questions 1–6

A motel operator is scheduling appointments to start up services at a new motel. Appointments for six services— gas, landscaping, power, satellite, telephone, and water—will be scheduled, one appointment per day for the next six days. The schedule for the appointments is subject to the following conditions:

The water appointment must be scheduled for an earlier day than the landscaping appointment.

The power appointment must be scheduled for an earlier day than both the gas and satellite appointments.

The appointments scheduled for the second and third days cannot be for either gas, satellite, or telephone.

The telephone appointment cannot be scheduled for the sixth day.

1. Which one of the following is an acceptable schedule of appointments, listed in order from earliest to latest?

   (A) gas, water, power, telephone, landscaping, satellite
   (B) power, water, landscaping, gas, satellite, telephone
   (C) telephone, power, landscaping, gas, water, satellite
   (D) telephone, water, power, landscaping, gas, satellite
   (E) water, telephone, power, gas, satellite, landscaping

2. If neither the gas nor the satellite nor the telephone appointment is scheduled for the fourth day, which one of the following must be true?

   (A) The gas appointment is scheduled for the fifth day.
   (B) The power appointment is scheduled for the third day.
   (C) The satellite appointment is scheduled for the sixth day.
   (D) The telephone appointment is scheduled for the first day.
   (E) The water appointment is scheduled for the second day.

3. Which one of the following must be true?

   (A) The landscaping appointment is scheduled for an earlier day than the telephone appointment.
   (B) The power appointment is scheduled for an earlier day than the landscaping appointment.
   (C) The telephone appointment is scheduled for an earlier day than the gas appointment.
   (D) The telephone appointment is scheduled for an earlier day than the water appointment.
   (E) The water appointment is scheduled for an earlier day than the gas appointment.

4. Which one of the following CANNOT be the appointments scheduled for the fourth, fifth, and sixth days, listed in that order?

   (A) gas, satellite, landscaping
   (B) landscaping, satellite, gas
   (C) power, satellite, gas
   (D) telephone, satellite, gas
   (E) water, gas, landscaping

5. If neither the gas appointment nor the satellite appointment is scheduled for the sixth day, which one of the following must be true?

   (A) The gas appointment is scheduled for the fifth day.
   (B) The landscaping appointment is scheduled for the sixth day.
   (C) The power appointment is scheduled for the third day.
   (D) The telephone appointment is scheduled for the fourth day.
   (E) The water appointment is scheduled for the second day.

6. Which one of the following, if substituted for the condition that the telephone appointment cannot be scheduled for the sixth day, would have the same effect in determining the order of the appointments?

   (A) The telephone appointment must be scheduled for an earlier day than the gas appointment or the satellite appointment, or both.
   (B) The telephone appointment must be scheduled for the day immediately before either the gas appointment or the satellite appointment.
   (C) The telephone appointment must be scheduled for an earlier day than the landscaping appointment.
   (D) If the telephone appointment is not scheduled for the first day, it must be scheduled for the day immediately before the gas appointment.
   (E) Either the gas appointment or the satellite appointment must be scheduled for the sixth day.

GO ON TO THE NEXT PAGE.

Questions 7–13

An artisan has been hired to create three stained glass windows. The artisan will use exactly five colors of glass: green, orange, purple, rose, and yellow. Each color of glass will be used at least once, and each window will contain at least two different colors of glass. The windows must also conform to the following conditions:

Exactly one of the windows contains both green glass and purple glass.

Exactly two of the windows contain rose glass.

If a window contains yellow glass, then that window contains neither green glass nor orange glass.

If a window does not contain purple glass, then that window contains orange glass.

7. Which one of the following could be the color combinations of the glass in the three windows?

(A) window 1: green, purple, rose, and orange
     window 2: rose and yellow
     window 3: green and orange
(B) window 1: green, purple, and rose
     window 2: green, rose, and orange
     window 3: purple and yellow
(C) window 1: green, purple, and rose
     window 2: green, purple, and orange
     window 3: purple, rose, and yellow
(D) window 1: green, purple, and orange
     window 2: rose, orange, and yellow
     window 3: purple and rose
(E) window 1: green, purple, and orange
     window 2: purple, rose, and yellow
     window 3: purple and orange

8. Which one of the following CANNOT be the complete color combination of the glass in one of the windows?

(A) green and orange
(B) green and purple
(C) green and rose
(D) purple and orange
(E) rose and orange

9. If two of the windows are made with exactly two colors of glass each, then the complete color combination of the glass in one of those windows could be

(A) rose and yellow
(B) orange and rose
(C) orange and purple
(D) green and rose
(E) green and orange

10. If the complete color combination of the glass in one of the windows is purple, rose, and orange, then the complete color combination of the glass in one of the other windows could be

(A) green, orange, and rose
(B) green, orange, and purple
(C) orange and rose
(D) orange and purple
(E) green and orange

11. If orange glass is used in more of the windows than green glass, then the complete color combination of the glass in one of the windows could be

(A) orange and purple
(B) green, purple, and rose
(C) green and purple
(D) green and orange
(E) green, orange, and rose

12. Which one of the following could be used in all three windows?

(A) green glass
(B) orange glass
(C) purple glass
(D) rose glass
(E) yellow glass

13. If none of the windows contains both rose glass and orange glass, then the complete color combination of the glass in one of the windows must be

(A) green and purple
(B) green, purple, and orange
(C) green and orange
(D) purple and orange
(E) purple, rose, and yellow

GO ON TO THE NEXT PAGE.

Questions 14–18

A conference on management skills consists of exactly five talks, which are held successively in the following order: Feedback, Goal Sharing, Handling People, Information Overload, and Leadership. Exactly four employees of SoftCorp—Quigley, Rivera, Spivey, and Tran—each attend exactly two of the talks. No talk is attended by more than two of the employees, who attend the talks in accordance with the following conditions:

Quigley attends neither Feedback nor Handling People.
Rivera attends neither Goal Sharing nor Handling People.
Spivey does not attend either of the talks that Tran attends.
Quigley attends the first talk Tran attends.
Spivey attends the first talk Rivera attends.

14. Which one of the following could be a complete and accurate matching of the talks to the SoftCorp employees who attend them?

(A) Feedback: Rivera, Spivey
     Goal Sharing: Quigley, Tran
     Handling People: None
     Information Overload: Quigley, Rivera
     Leadership: Spivey, Tran
(B) Feedback: Rivera, Spivey
     Goal Sharing: Quigley, Tran
     Handling People: Rivera, Tran
     Information Overload: Quigley
     Leadership: Spivey
(C) Feedback: Rivera, Spivey
     Goal Sharing: Quigley, Tran
     Handling People: Tran
     Information Overload: Quigley, Rivera
     Leadership: Spivey
(D) Feedback: Rivera, Spivey
     Goal Sharing: Tran
     Handling People: Tran
     Information Overload: Quigley, Rivera
     Leadership: Quigley, Spivey
(E) Feedback: Spivey
     Goal Sharing: Quigley, Tran
     Handling People: Spivey
     Information Overload: Quigley, Rivera
     Leadership: Rivera, Tran

15. If none of the SoftCorp employees attends Handling People, then which one of the following must be true?

(A) Rivera attends Feedback.
(B) Rivera attends Leadership.
(C) Spivey attends Information Overload.
(D) Tran attends Goal Sharing.
(E) Tran attends Information Overload.

16. Which one of the following is a complete and accurate list of the talks any one of which Rivera and Spivey could attend together?

(A) Feedback, Information Overload, Leadership
(B) Feedback, Goal Sharing, Information Overload
(C) Information Overload, Leadership
(D) Feedback, Leadership
(E) Feedback, Information Overload

17. If Quigley is the only SoftCorp employee to attend Leadership, then which one of the following could be false?

(A) Rivera attends Feedback.
(B) Rivera attends Information Overload.
(C) Spivey attends Feedback.
(D) Spivey attends Handling People.
(E) Tran attends Goal Sharing.

18. If Rivera is the only SoftCorp employee to attend Information Overload, then which one of the following could be false?

(A) Quigley attends Leadership.
(B) Rivera attends Feedback.
(C) Spivey attends Feedback.
(D) Tran attends Goal Sharing.
(E) Tran attends Handling People.

GO ON TO THE NEXT PAGE.

Questions 19–23

Exactly six witnesses will testify in a trial: Mangione, Ramirez, Sanderson, Tannenbaum, Ujemori, and Wong. The witnesses will testify one by one, and each only once. The order in which the witnesses testify is subject to the following constraints:

Sanderson must testify immediately before either Tannenbaum or Ujemori.

Ujemori must testify earlier than both Ramirez and Wong.

Either Tannenbaum or Wong must testify immediately before Mangione.

19. Which one of the following lists the witnesses in an order in which they could testify?

(A) Ramirez, Sanderson, Tannenbaum, Mangione, Ujemori, Wong

(B) Sanderson, Tannenbaum, Ujemori, Ramirez, Wong, Mangione

(C) Sanderson, Ujemori, Tannenbaum, Wong, Ramirez, Mangione

(D) Tannenbaum, Mangione, Ujemori, Sanderson, Ramirez, Wong

(E) Wong, Ramirez, Sanderson, Tannenbaum, Mangione, Ujemori

20. If Tannenbaum testifies first, then which one of the following could be true?

(A) Ramirez testifies second.
(B) Wong testifies third.
(C) Sanderson testifies fourth.
(D) Ujemori testifies fifth.
(E) Mangione testifies sixth.

21. If Sanderson testifies fifth, then Ujemori must testify

(A) first
(B) second
(C) third
(D) fourth
(E) sixth

22. Which one of the following pairs of witnesses CANNOT testify third and fourth, respectively?

(A) Mangione, Tannenbaum
(B) Ramirez, Sanderson
(C) Sanderson, Ujemori
(D) Tannenbaum, Ramirez
(E) Ujemori, Wong

23. Which one of the following pairs of witnesses CANNOT testify first and second, respectively?

(A) Sanderson, Ujemori
(B) Tannenbaum, Mangione
(C) Tannenbaum, Sanderson
(D) Ujemori, Tannenbaum
(E) Ujemori, Wong

S T O P

IF YOU FINISH BEFORE TIME IS CALLED, YOU MAY CHECK YOUR WORK ON THIS SECTION ONLY.
DO NOT WORK ON ANY OTHER SECTION IN THE TEST.

SECTION IV

Time—35 minutes

26 Questions

<u>Directions:</u> The questions in this section are based on the reasoning contained in brief statements or passages. For some questions, more than one of the choices could conceivably answer the question. However, you are to choose the <u>best</u> answer; that is, the response that most accurately and completely answers the question. You should not make assumptions that are by commonsense standards implausible, superfluous, or incompatible with the passage. After you have chosen the best answer, blacken the corresponding space on your answer sheet.

1. Marine biologist: Scientists have long wondered why the fish that live around coral reefs exhibit such brilliant colors. One suggestion is that coral reefs are colorful and, therefore, that colorful fish are camouflaged by them. Many animal species, after all, use camouflage to avoid predators. However, as regards the populations around reefs, this suggestion is mistaken. A reef stripped of its fish is quite monochromatic. Most corals, it turns out, are relatively dull browns and greens.

Which one of the following most accurately expresses the main conclusion drawn in the marine biologist's argument?

(A) One hypothesis about why fish living near coral reefs exhibit such bright colors is that the fish are camouflaged by their bright colors.

(B) The fact that many species use camouflage to avoid predators is one reason to believe that brightly colored fish living near reefs do too.

(C) The suggestion that the fish living around coral reefs exhibit bright colors because they are camouflaged by the reefs is mistaken.

(D) A reef stripped of its fish is relatively monochromatic.

(E) It turns out that the corals in a coral reef are mostly dull hues of brown and green.

2. To discover what percentage of teenagers believe in telekinesis—the psychic ability to move objects without physically touching them—a recent survey asked a representative sample of teenagers whether they agreed with the following statement: "A person's thoughts can influence the movement of physical objects." But because this statement is particularly ambiguous and is amenable to a naturalistic, uncontroversial interpretation, the survey's responses are also ambiguous.

The reasoning above conforms most closely to which one of the following general propositions?

(A) Uncontroversial statements are useless in surveys.

(B) Every statement is amenable to several interpretations.

(C) Responses to surveys are always unambiguous if the survey's questions are well phrased.

(D) Responses people give to poorly phrased questions are likely to be ambiguous.

(E) Statements about psychic phenomena can always be given naturalistic interpretations.

GO ON TO THE NEXT PAGE.

3. A recent study of perfect pitch—the ability to identify the pitch of an isolated musical note—found that a high percentage of people who have perfect pitch are related to someone else who has it. Among those without perfect pitch, the percentage was much lower. This shows that having perfect pitch is a consequence of genetic factors.

Which one of the following, if true, most strengthens the argument?

(A) People who have relatives with perfect pitch generally receive no more musical training than do others.

(B) All of the researchers conducting the study had perfect pitch.

(C) People with perfect pitch are more likely than others to choose music as a career.

(D) People with perfect pitch are more likely than others to make sure that their children receive musical training.

(E) People who have some training in music are more likely to have perfect pitch than those with no such training.

4. Paleontologists recently excavated two corresponding sets of dinosaur tracks, one left by a large grazing dinosaur and the other by a smaller predatory dinosaur. The two sets of tracks make abrupt turns repeatedly in tandem, suggesting that the predator was following the grazing dinosaur and had matched its stride. Modern predatory mammals, such as lions, usually match the stride of prey they are chasing immediately before they strike those prey. This suggests that the predatory dinosaur was chasing the grazing dinosaur and attacked immediately afterwards.

Which one of the following most accurately describes the role played in the argument by the statement that the predatory dinosaur was following the grazing dinosaur and had matched its stride?

(A) It helps establish the scientific importance of the argument's overall conclusion, but is not offered as evidence for that conclusion.

(B) It is a hypothesis that is rejected in favor of the hypothesis stated in the argument's overall conclusion.

(C) It provides the basis for an analogy used in support of the argument's overall conclusion.

(D) It is presented to counteract a possible objection to the argument's overall conclusion.

(E) It is the overall conclusion of the argument.

5. Researchers announced recently that over the past 25 years the incidence of skin cancer caused by exposure to harmful rays from the sun has continued to grow in spite of the increasingly widespread use of sunscreens. This shows that using sunscreen is unlikely to reduce a person's risk of developing such skin cancer.

Which one of the following, if true, most weakens the argument?

(A) Most people who purchase a sunscreen product will not purchase the most expensive brand available.

(B) Skin cancer generally develops among the very old as a result of sunburns experienced when very young.

(C) The development of sunscreens by pharmaceutical companies was based upon research conducted by dermatologists.

(D) People who know that they are especially susceptible to skin cancer are generally disinclined to spend a large amount of time in the sun.

(E) Those who use sunscreens most regularly are people who believe themselves to be most susceptible to skin cancer.

6. University administrator: Any proposal for a new department will not be funded if there are fewer than 50 people per year available for hire in that field and the proposed department would duplicate more than 25 percent of the material covered in one of our existing departments. The proposed Area Studies Department will duplicate more than 25 percent of the material covered in our existing Anthropology Department. However, we will fund the new department.

Which one of the following statements follows logically from the university administrator's statements?

(A) The field of Area Studies has at least 50 people per year available for hire.

(B) The proposed Area Studies Department would not duplicate more than 25 percent of the material covered in any existing department other than Anthropology.

(C) If the proposed Area Studies Department did not duplicate more than 25 percent of the material covered in Anthropology, then the new department would not be funded.

(D) The Anthropology Department duplicates more than 25 percent of the material covered in the proposed Area Studies Department.

(E) The field of Area Studies has fewer than 50 people per year available for hire.

GO ON TO THE NEXT PAGE.

7. Researcher: Over the course of three decades, we kept records of the average beak size of two populations of the same species of bird, one wild population, the other captive. During this period, the average beak size of the captive birds did not change, while the average beak size of the wild birds decreased significantly.

    Which one of the following, if true, most helps to explain the researcher's findings?

    (A)   The small-beaked wild birds were easier to capture and measure than the large-beaked wild birds.
    (B)   The large-beaked wild birds were easier to capture and measure than the small-beaked wild birds.
    (C)   Changes in the wild birds' food supply during the study period favored the survival of small-beaked birds over large-beaked birds.
    (D)   The average body size of the captive birds remained the same over the study period.
    (E)   The researcher measured the beaks of some of the wild birds on more than one occasion.

8. Storytelling appears to be a universal aspect of both past and present cultures. Comparative study of traditional narratives from widely separated epochs and diverse cultures reveals common themes such as creation, tribal origin, mystical beings and quasi-historical figures, and common story types such as fables and tales in which animals assume human personalities.

    The evidence cited above from the study of traditional narratives most supports which one of the following statements?

    (A)   Storytellers routinely borrow themes from other cultures.
    (B)   Storytellers have long understood that the narrative is a universal aspect of human culture.
    (C)   Certain human concerns and interests arise in all of the world's cultures.
    (D)   Storytelling was no less important in ancient cultures than it is in modern cultures.
    (E)   The best way to understand a culture is to understand what motivates its storytellers.

9. If a mother's first child is born before its due date, it is likely that her second child will be also. Jackie's second child was not born before its due date, so it is likely that Jackie's first child was not born before its due date either.

    The questionable reasoning in the argument above is most similar in its reasoning to which one of the following?

    (A)   Artisans who finish their projects before the craft fair will probably go to the craft fair. Ben will not finish his project before the fair. So he probably will not go to the craft fair.
    (B)   All responsible pet owners are likely to be good with children. So anyone who is good with children is probably a responsible pet owner.
    (C)   If a movie is a box-office hit, it is likely that its sequel will be also. *Hawkman II*, the sequel to *Hawkman I*, was not a box-office hit, so *Hawkman I* was probably not a box-office hit.
    (D)   If a business is likely to fail, people will not invest in it. Pallid Starr is likely to fail, therefore no one is likely to invest in it.
    (E)   Tai will go sailing only if the weather is nice. The weather will be nice, thus Tai will probably go sailing.

10. Science journalist: Europa, a moon of Jupiter, is covered with ice. Data recently transmitted by a spacecraft strongly suggest that there are oceans of liquid water deep under the ice. Life as we know it could evolve only in the presence of liquid water. Hence, it is likely that at least primitive life has evolved on Europa.

    The science journalist's argument is most vulnerable to criticism on the grounds that it

    (A)   takes for granted that if a condition would be necessary for the evolution of life as we know it, then such life could not have evolved anywhere that this condition does not hold
    (B)   fails to address adequately the possibility that there are conditions necessary for the evolution of life in addition to the presence of liquid water
    (C)   takes for granted that life is likely to be present on Europa if, but only if, life evolved on Europa
    (D)   overlooks the possibility that there could be unfamiliar forms of life that have evolved without the presence of liquid water
    (E)   takes for granted that no conditions on Europa other than the supposed presence of liquid water could have accounted for the data transmitted by the spacecraft

GO ON TO THE NEXT PAGE.

11. A bacterial species will inevitably develop greater resistance within a few years to any antibiotics used against it, unless those antibiotics eliminate that species completely. However, no single antibiotic now on the market is powerful enough to eliminate bacterial species X completely.

Which one of the following is most strongly supported by the statements above?

(A) It is unlikely that any antibiotic can be developed that will completely eliminate bacterial species X.

(B) If any antibiotic now on the market is used against bacterial species X, that species will develop greater resistance to it within a few years.

(C) The only way of completely eliminating bacterial species X is by a combination of two or more antibiotics now on the market.

(D) Bacterial species X will inevitably become more virulent in the course of time.

(E) Bacterial species X is more resistant to at least some antibiotics that have been used against it than it was before those antibiotics were used against it.

12. Political scientist: It is not uncommon for a politician to criticize his or her political opponents by claiming that their exposition of their ideas is muddled and incomprehensible. Such criticism, however, is never sincere. Political agendas promoted in a manner that cannot be understood by large numbers of people will not be realized for, as every politician knows, political mobilization requires commonality of purpose.

Which one of the following is the most accurate rendering of the political scientist's main conclusion?

(A) People who promote political agendas in an incomprehensible manner should be regarded as insincere.

(B) Sincere critics of the proponents of a political agenda should not focus their criticisms on the manner in which that agenda is promoted.

(C) The ineffectiveness of a confusingly promoted political agenda is a reason for refraining from, rather than engaging in, criticism of those who are promoting it.

(D) A politician criticizing his or her political opponents for presenting their political agendas in an incomprehensible manner is being insincere.

(E) To mobilize large numbers of people in support of a political agenda, that political agenda must be presented in such a way that it cannot be misunderstood.

13. Many symptoms of mental illnesses are affected by organic factors such as a deficiency in a compound in the brain. What is surprising, however, is the tremendous variation among different countries in the incidence of these symptoms in people with mental illnesses. This variation establishes that the organic factors that affect symptoms of mental illnesses are not distributed evenly around the globe.

The reasoning above is most vulnerable to criticism on the grounds that it

(A) does not say how many different mental illnesses are being discussed

(B) neglects the possibility that nutritional factors that contribute to deficiencies in compounds in the brain vary from culture to culture

(C) fails to consider the possibility that cultural factors significantly affect how mental illnesses manifest themselves in symptoms

(D) presumes, without providing justification, that any change in brain chemistry manifests itself as a change in mental condition

(E) presumes, without providing justification, that mental phenomena are only manifestations of physical phenomena

14. Politician: It has been proposed that the national parks in our country be managed by private companies rather than the government. A similar privatization of the telecommunications industry has benefited consumers by allowing competition among a variety of telephone companies to improve service and force down prices. Therefore, the privatization of the national parks would probably benefit park visitors as well.

Which one of the following, if true, most weakens the politician's argument?

(A) It would not be politically expedient to privatize the national parks even if doing so would, in the long run, improve service and reduce the fees charged to visitors.

(B) The privatization of the telecommunications industry has been problematic in that it has led to significantly increased unemployment and economic instability in that industry.

(C) The vast majority of people visiting the national parks are unaware of proposals to privatize the management of those parks.

(D) Privatizing the national parks would benefit a much smaller number of consumers to a much smaller extent than did the privatization of the telecommunications industry.

(E) The privatization of the national parks would produce much less competition between different companies than did the privatization of the telecommunications industry.

GO ON TO THE NEXT PAGE.

15. Jewel collectors, fearing that their eyes will be deceived by a counterfeit, will not buy a diamond unless the dealer guarantees that it is genuine. But why should a counterfeit give any less aesthetic pleasure when the naked eye cannot distinguish it from a real diamond? Both jewels should be deemed of equal value.

Which one of the following principles, if valid, most helps to justify the reasoning in the argument above?

(A) Jewel collectors should collect only those jewels that provide the most aesthetic pleasure.

(B) The value of a jewel should depend at least partly on market demand.

(C) It should not be assumed that everyone who likes diamonds receives the same degree of aesthetic pleasure from them.

(D) The value of a jewel should derive solely from the aesthetic pleasure it provides.

(E) Jewel collectors should not buy counterfeit jewels unless they are unable to distinguish counterfeit jewels from real ones.

16. All etching tools are either pin-tipped or bladed. While some bladed etching tools are used for engraving, some are not. On the other hand, all pin-tipped etching tools are used for engraving. Thus, there are more etching tools that are used for engraving than there are etching tools that are not used for engraving.

The conclusion of the argument follows logically if which one of the following is assumed?

(A) All tools used for engraving are etching tools as well.

(B) There are as many pin-tipped etching tools as there are bladed etching tools.

(C) No etching tool is both pin-tipped and bladed.

(D) The majority of bladed etching tools are not used for engraving.

(E) All etching tools that are not used for engraving are bladed.

17. A 24-year study of 1,500 adults showed that those subjects with a high intake of foods rich in beta-carotene were much less likely to die from cancer or heart disease than were those with a low intake of such foods. On the other hand, taking beta-carotene supplements for 12 years had no positive or negative effect on the health of subjects in a separate study of 20,000 adults.

Each of the following, if true, would help to resolve the apparent discrepancy between the results of the two studies EXCEPT:

(A) The human body processes the beta-carotene present in foods much more efficiently than it does beta-carotene supplements.

(B) Beta-carotene must be taken for longer than 12 years to have any cancer-preventive effects.

(C) Foods rich in beta-carotene also tend to contain other nutrients that assist in the human body's absorption of beta-carotene.

(D) In the 12-year study, half of the subjects were given beta-carotene supplements and half were given a placebo.

(E) In the 24-year study, the percentage of the subjects who had a high intake of beta-carotene-rich foods who smoked cigarettes was much smaller than the percentage of the subjects with a low intake of beta-carotene-rich foods who smoked.

GO ON TO THE NEXT PAGE.

18. If there are sentient beings on planets outside our solar system, we will not be able to determine this anytime in the near future unless some of these beings are at least as intelligent as humans. We will not be able to send spacecraft to planets outside our solar system anytime in the near future, and any sentient being on another planet capable of communicating with us anytime in the near future would have to be at least as intelligent as we are.

The argument's conclusion can be properly inferred if which one of the following is assumed?

(A) There are no sentient beings on planets in our solar system other than those on Earth.

(B) Any beings that are at least as intelligent as humans would want to communicate with sentient beings outside their own solar systems.

(C) If there is a sentient being on another planet that is as intelligent as humans are, we will not be able to send spacecraft to the being's planet anytime in the near future.

(D) If a sentient being on another planet cannot communicate with us, then the only way to detect its existence is by sending a spacecraft to its planet.

(E) Any sentient beings on planets outside our solar system that are at least as intelligent as humans would be capable of communicating with us.

19. Doctor: Medical researchers recently examined a large group of individuals who said that they had never experienced serious back pain. Half of the members of the group turned out to have bulging or slipped disks in their spines, conditions often blamed for serious back pain. Since these individuals with bulging or slipped disks evidently felt no pain from them, these conditions could not lead to serious back pain in people who do experience such pain.

The reasoning in the doctor's argument is most vulnerable to the criticism that it fails to consider which one of the following possibilities?

(A) A factor that need not be present in order for a certain effect to arise may nonetheless be sufficient to produce that effect.

(B) A factor that is not in itself sufficient to produce a certain effect may nonetheless be partly responsible for that effect in some instances.

(C) An effect that occurs in the absence of a particular phenomenon might not occur when that phenomenon is present.

(D) A characteristic found in half of a given sample of the population might not occur in half of the entire population.

(E) A factor that does not bring about a certain effect may nonetheless be more likely to be present when the effect occurs than when the effect does not occur.

20. Many workers who handled substance T in factories became seriously ill years later. We now know T caused at least some of their illnesses. Earlier ignorance of this connection does not absolve T's manufacturer of all responsibility. For had it investigated the safety of T before allowing workers to be exposed to it, many of their illnesses would have been prevented.

Which one of the following principles most helps to justify the conclusion above?

(A) Employees who are harmed by substances they handle on the job should be compensated for medical costs they incur as a result.

(B) Manufacturers should be held responsible only for the preventable consequences of their actions.

(C) Manufacturers have an obligation to inform workers of health risks of which they are aware.

(D) Whether or not an action's consequences were preventable is irrelevant to whether a manufacturer should be held responsible for those consequences.

(E) Manufacturers should be held responsible for the consequences of any of their actions that harm innocent people if those consequences were preventable.

21. It is virtually certain that the government contract for building the new highway will be awarded to either Phoenix Contracting or Cartwright Company. I have just learned that the government has decided not to award the contract to Cartwright Company. It is therefore almost inevitable that Phoenix Contracting will be awarded the contract.

The argument proceeds by

(A) concluding that it is extremely likely that an event will occur by ruling out the only probable alternative

(B) inferring, from a claim that one of two possible events will occur, that the other event will not occur

(C) refuting a claim that a particular event is inevitable by establishing the possibility of an alternative event

(D) predicting a future event on the basis of an established pattern of past events

(E) inferring a claim about the probability of a particular event from a general statistical statement

GO ON TO THE NEXT PAGE.

22. Researchers have found that children in large families—particularly the younger siblings—generally have fewer allergies than children in small families do. They hypothesize that exposure to germs during infancy makes people less likely to develop allergies.

Which one of the following, if true, most supports the researchers' hypothesis?

(A) In countries where the average number of children per family has decreased over the last century, the incidence of allergies has increased.
(B) Children in small families generally eat more kinds of very allergenic foods than children in large families do.
(C) Some allergies are life threatening, while many diseases caused by germs produce only temporary discomfort.
(D) Children whose parents have allergies have an above-average likelihood of developing allergies themselves.
(E) Children from small families who entered day care before age one were less likely to develop allergies than children from small families who entered day care later.

23. Film preservation requires transferring old movies from their original material—unstable, deteriorating nitrate film—to stable acetate film. But this is a time-consuming, expensive process, and there is no way to transfer all currently deteriorating nitrate films to acetate before they disintegrate. So some films from the earliest years of Hollywood will not be preserved.

Which one of the following is an assumption on which the argument depends?

(A) No new technology for transferring old movies from nitrate film to acetate film will ever be developed.
(B) Transferring films from nitrate to acetate is not the least expensive way of preserving them.
(C) Not many films from the earliest years of Hollywood have already been transferred to acetate.
(D) Some films from the earliest years of Hollywood currently exist solely in their original material.
(E) The least popular films from the earliest years of Hollywood are the ones most likely to be lost.

24. In a recent study of arthritis, researchers tried but failed to find any correlation between pain intensity and any of those features of the weather—humidity, temperature swings, barometric pressure—usually cited by arthritis sufferers as the cause of their increased pain. Those arthritis sufferers in the study who were convinced of the existence of such a correlation gave widely varying accounts of the time delay between the occurrence of what they believed to be the relevant feature of the weather and the increased intensity of the pain. Thus, this study _____.

Of the following, which one most logically completes the argument?

(A) indicates that the weather affects some arthritis sufferers more quickly than it does other arthritis sufferers
(B) indicates that arthritis sufferers' beliefs about the causes of the pain they feel may affect their assessment of the intensity of that pain
(C) suggests that arthritis sufferers are imagining the correlation they assert to exist
(D) suggests that some people are more susceptible to weather-induced arthritis pain than are others
(E) suggests that the scientific investigation of possible links between weather and arthritis pain is impossible

GO ON TO THE NEXT PAGE.

25. Cities with healthy economies typically have plenty of job openings. Cities with high-technology businesses also tend to have healthy economies, so those in search of jobs should move to a city with high-technology businesses.

The reasoning in which one of the following is most similar to the reasoning in the argument above?

(A)   Older antiques are usually the most valuable. Antique dealers generally authenticate the age of the antiques they sell, so those collectors who want the most valuable antiques should purchase their antiques from antique dealers.

(B)   Antique dealers who authenticate the age of the antiques they sell typically have plenty of antiques for sale. Since the most valuable antiques are those that have had their ages authenticated, antique collectors in search of valuable antiques should purchase their antiques from antique dealers.

(C)   Antiques that have had their ages authenticated tend to be valuable. Since antique dealers generally carry antiques that have had their ages authenticated, those collectors who want antiques that are valuable should purchase their antiques from antique dealers.

(D)   Many antique collectors know that antique dealers can authenticate the age of the antiques they sell. Since antiques that have had their ages authenticated are always the most valuable, most antique collectors who want antiques that are valuable tend to purchase their antiques from antique dealers.

(E)   Many antiques increase in value once they have had their ages authenticated by antique dealers. Since antique dealers tend to have plenty of valuable antiques, antique collectors who prefer to purchase the most valuable antiques should purchase antiques from antique dealers.

26. Sociologist: A recent study of 5,000 individuals found, on the basis of a physical exam, that more than 25 percent of people older than 65 were malnourished, though only 12 percent of the people in this age group fell below government poverty standards. In contrast, a greater percentage of the people 65 or younger fell below poverty standards than were found in the study to be malnourished.

Each of the following, if true, helps to explain the findings of the study cited by the sociologist EXCEPT:

(A)   Doctors are less likely to correctly diagnose and treat malnutrition in their patients who are over 65 than in their younger patients.

(B)   People over 65 are more likely to take medications that increase their need for certain nutrients than are people 65 or younger.

(C)   People over 65 are more likely to suffer from loss of appetite due to medication than are people 65 or younger.

(D)   People 65 or younger are no more likely to fall below government poverty standards than are people over 65.

(E)   People 65 or younger are less likely to have medical conditions that interfere with their digestion than are people over 65.

S T O P

IF YOU FINISH BEFORE TIME IS CALLED, YOU MAY CHECK YOUR WORK ON THIS SECTION ONLY.
DO NOT WORK ON ANY OTHER SECTION IN THE TEST.

Acknowledgment is made to the following sources from which material has been adapted for use in this test booklet:

Richard H. Brodhead, *Cultures of Letters: Scenes of Reading and Writing in Nineteenth-Century America.* ©1993 by the University of Chicago.

Jonathan Glater and Alan Finder, "In Tuition Game, Popularity Rises with Price." ©December 12, 2006 by The New York Times.

Josie Glausiusz, "Seismologists Go Green." ©1999 by the Walt Disney Company.

Michael Pietrusewsky and Michele Toomay Douglas, "Intensification of Agriculture at Ban Chiang: Is There Evidence from the Skeletons?" ©2001 by University of Hawaii Press.

Karen Gust Schollmeyer and Christy G. Turner II, "Dental Caries, Prehistoric Diet, and the Pithouse-to-Pueblo Transition in Southwestern Colorado." ©2004 by Society for American Archaeology.

Wait for the supervisor's instructions before you open the page to the topic.
Please print and sign your name and write the date in the designated spaces below.

Time: 35 Minutes

General Directions

u will have 35 minutes in which to plan and write an essay on the topic inside. Read the topic and the accompanying directions carefully. u will probably find it best to spend a few minutes considering the topic and organizing your thoughts before you begin writing. In your essay, sure to develop your ideas fully, leaving time, if possible, to review what you have written. **Do not write on a topic other than the one ecified. Writing on a topic of your own choice is not acceptable.**

special knowledge is required or expected for this writing exercise. Law schools are interested in the reasoning, clarity, organization, guage usage, and writing mechanics displayed in your essay. How well you write is more important than how much you write.

fine your essay to the blocked, lined area on the front and back of the separate Writing Sample Response Sheet. Only that area will be roduced for law schools. Be sure that your writing is legible.

Both this topic sheet and your response sheet must be turned over to the testing staff before you leave the room.

Topic Code	Print Your Full Name Here		
095316	Last	First	M.I.

Date	Sign Your Name Here
/ /	

Scratch Paper
Do not write your essay in this space.

LSAT® Writing Sample Topic

Directions: The scenario presented below describes two choices, either one of which can be supported on the basis of the information given. Your essay should consider both choices and argue for one over the other, based on the two specified criteria and the facts provided. There is no "right" or "wrong" choice: a reasonable argument can be made for either.

The Wangs must arrange summer child care for their ten-year-old child. They have found two summer-long programs that are affordabl and in which friends of their child would also be participating. Using the facts below, write an essay in which you argue for one program over t other based on the following two considerations:

- The Wangs want their child to enjoy activities that would add variety to the regular school experience.
- Transportation to the program must be easy for the Wangs to accommodate to their work situations.

City Summer is located at a college near Mrs. Wang's job but a considerable distance from Mr. Wang's. It offers early arrival and late pick-up times for parent convenience. Mrs. Wang has somewhat flexible work hours, but must travel overnight occasionally. City Summer offers classes in the visual arts, dance, drama, music, swimming, and gymnastics, as well as gym activities like basketball and volleyball. In addition, there are organized field trips to museums, plays, and historical sites. The program concludes with a presentation of student work from the classes.

Round Lake Camp is located 30 minutes outside the city. Bus transportation is provided to and from several city schools, one of which next door to Mr. Wang's job. Pick-up and drop-off are at set times in the early morning and late afternoon. Mr. Wang has flexibility in his work starting time but often must work late. The camp has classes in swimming, sailing, archery, nature study, crafts, and outdoor skills. It also has regular free periods when campers can choose among outdoor activities or just explore the woods. At the end of the summer the campers ha an overnight camping trip at a nearby state wilderness area.

WP-RC

Scratch Paper
Do not write your essay in this space.

LAST NAME (Print)

FIRST NAME (Print)

SSN/ SIN

L

LSAC ACCOUNT NO.

MI

TEST CENTER NO.

SIGNATURE

M M D D Y
TEST DATE

TOPIC CODE

Writing Sample Response Sheet

DO NOT WRITE IN THIS SPACE

Begin your essay in the lined area below.
Continue on the back if you need more space.

COMPUTING YOUR SCORE

Directions:

1. Use the Answer Key on the next page to check your answers.

2. Use the Scoring Worksheet below to compute your raw score.

3. Use the Score Conversion Chart to convert your raw score into the 120–180 scale.

Scoring Worksheet

1. Enter the number of questions you answered correctly in each section.

	Number Correct
SECTION I.................	_____
SECTION II...............	_____
SECTION III..............	_____
SECTION IV	_____

2. Enter the sum here: _____
   This is your Raw Score.

Conversion Chart
For Converting Raw Score to the 120–180 LSAT Scaled Score
LSAT Form 0LSN85

Reported Score	Raw Score Lowest	Raw Score Highest
180	99	102
179	98	98
178	97	97
177	96	96
176	95	95
175	94	94
174	93	93
173	91	92
172	90	90
171	89	89
170	88	88
169	86	87
168	85	85
167	83	84
166	82	82
165	80	81
164	79	79
163	77	78
162	75	76
161	74	74
160	72	73
159	70	71
158	69	69
157	67	68
156	65	66
155	63	64
154	62	62
153	60	61
152	58	59
151	57	57
150	55	56
149	53	54
148	52	52
147	50	51
146	48	49
145	47	47
144	45	46
143	43	44
142	42	42
141	40	41
140	39	39
139	37	38
138	36	36
137	35	35
136	33	34
135	32	32
134	30	31
133	29	29
132	28	28
131	27	27
130	25	26
129	24	24
128	23	23
127	22	22
126	21	21
125	20	20
124	18	19
123	17	17
122	16	16
121	15	15
120	0	14

ANSWER KEY

SECTION I

1.	A	8.	D	15.	A	22.	D
2.	C	9.	A	16.	B	23.	C
3.	E	10.	E	17.	A	24.	B
4.	B	11.	E	18.	B	25.	E
5.	B	12.	D	19.	D	26.	E
6.	E	13.	C	20.	C	27.	C
7.	D	14.	B	21.	D		

SECTION II

1.	D	8.	A	15.	B	22.	D
2.	E	9.	C	16.	E	23.	C
3.	B	10.	B	17.	A	24.	E
4.	E	11.	A	18.	D	25.	A
5.	C	12.	E	19.	D	26.	E
6.	A	13.	D	20.	C		
7.	C	14.	B	21.	E		

SECTION III

1.	D	8.	C	15.	A	22.	A
2.	D	9.	B	16.	A	23.	D
3.	E	10.	B	17.	D		
4.	E	11.	A	18.	E		
5.	B	12.	C	19.	B		
6.	A	13.	E	20.	E		
7.	B	14.	C	21.	A		

SECTION IV

1.	C	8.	C	15.	D	22.	E
2.	D	9.	C	16.	B	23.	D
3.	A	10.	B	17.	D	24.	C
4.	C	11.	B	18.	D	25.	C
5.	B	12.	D	19.	B	26.	D
6.	A	13.	C	20.	E		
7.	C	14.	E	21.	A		

LSAT® PREP TOOLS

New! The Official LSAT Handbook

Get to know the LSAT

The LSAT is a test of analytical reasoning, logical reasoning, and reading comprehension, including comparative reading. What's the best way to learn how to approach these types of questions *before* you encounter them on the day of the test? There's no better way than The Official LSAT Handbook, published by the Law School Admission Council, the organization that produces the LSAT. This inexpensive guide will introduce you to the skills that the LSAT is designed to assess so that you can make the most of the rest of your test preparation and do your best on the test. (Note: This handbook contains information that is also included in The Official LSAT SuperPrep. The information in The Official LSAT Handbook has been expanded and updated since it was first published in The Official LSAT SuperPrep.)

$12 ($9.95 online)

LSAC.org